GunDigest

SHOOTER'S
GUIDE to **RIFLE**
MARKSMANSHIP

PETER LESSLER

Published by

Gun Digest® Books, an imprint of F+W Media, Inc.
Krause Publications • 700 East State Street • Iola, WI 54990-0001
715-445-2214 • 888-457-2873
www.krausebooks.com

To order books or other products call toll-free 1-800-258-0929
or visit us online at www.gundigeststore.com

ISBN-13: 978-1-4402-3512-2
ISBN-10: 1-4402-3512-0

Cover Design by Al West
Designed by Sandi Carpenter
Edited by Corrina Peterson

Featuring photos by Richard Gugeler of Ragtop Photography

Printed in the United States of America

DEDICATION

To my parents, who didn't bat an eye when I wanted to join the high school rifle team and NRA junior smallbore rifle club; to the late Lt. Col. Jeff Cooper, whose teachings helped make me a better shot and whose writings helped make me a better citizen and man; and to the late Eddie Rhodes, IPSC Grandmaster, three-gun champion, police captain, and outstanding man, who left us far too early, and whose smarts, wit, and big heart are greatly missed by many.

OLYMPEION
An Ode to the Rifle
by Lt. Col. Jeff Cooper

You hold in your hands the bow of Diana,
the spear of Achilles, the hammer of Thor.
Now you command both precision and distance.
To dominant power you've opened the door.

Your rifle embodies the gift of Hephaistos,
the grant of Olympus to hapless mankind.
Your rifle's a thing of both power and beauty.
It's proper employment ennobles the mind.

Bare-handed you live at the mercy of numbers,
but numbers can never match riflemen's skill.
Your rifle essentially makes you the master;
it creates and maintains humanities' will.

Vulcan has given you means to establish
divine domination o'er man, beast, and foe.
Your rifle's the sorcerous sceptre of power.
Direct it with wisdom and judgement bestow.

CONTENTS

I got my start in real rifle shooting on the smallbore rifle team of Parsippany High School, NJ, which had its own indoor basement 50-ft. rifle range; in the local NRA smallbore rifle club which used that same range; the Police Athletic League indoor range in Wayne, NJ; and the wonderful old P.J. O'Hare's target shooter's supply store and outdoor 50/100 yard range, now long gone.

Thanks to Parsippany team coach Roy Helmlinger, Mr. & Mrs. Wendland of the NRA and other instructors whose names I've forgotten over nearly 40 years, and a couple of good marksmanship books in the county library, I had a pretty good start. Added to that is the personal help of many highpower rifle competitive shooters including Roger Billington, Jim Starr, Jim Volk, and others; and the Cooper General Rifle course instructor cadre: Tom Russell, Mike Waidelich, and Rich Wyatt. Col. Cooper's teachings and writings, and the writings of highpower champion G. David Tubb and Randolph Constantine, helped greatly as well. My shooting partners Bob Dull, Richard Gugeler (who took the pictures here), and Paul Rademaker helped keep me from slacking off (with varying degrees of success) as well. And thanks to Jim Heath for creating the sight alignment/sight picture graphics.

Volunteering with the Appleseed Project has helped me become a far better and more efficient instructor than before. Attending their marksmanship/history clinic is something all Americans should experience.

Without the above guidance, I'd still be shooting mostly from the bench, and without the bench, having a hard time hitting the broad side of a barn from inside it. Thanks all.

"Good shooting is good execution of the fundamentals. Great shooting is great execution of the fundamentals."

I heard the coach of the Colorado state junior highpower rifle team say that at a highpower rifle bullseye clinic. Fundamentals are not some basic things you breeze by on your way to something more exciting. Rather, they are the foundation of everything you do when taking every shot. No matter what kind of shooting you do, if your fundamentals are incomplete or poorly performed, your shooting will suffer.

Whether beginning shooter or experienced competitor, you will find plenty of useful information here, since much that will be covered has not made it out into the general shooting population. Let me also state that this book is not about tactics, nor concealed carry, nor close-quarters battle techniques, nor various shooting sports, etc. This book is about marksmanship: how to hit with consistent accuracy, and to do so quickly. It is also not about going from say, expert level to master level – though it might help some. It is about making sure that your foundational skills are complete and correct, giving you a solid platform from which to pursue further progress.

The rifle is primarily an offensive arm allowing devastating power to be delivered, with range and precision limited only by the power of the cartridge and skill of the user. With this in mind, the purpose of this book is to teach the fundamental skills of rifle shooting to those who have not been formally trained in or otherwise exposed to the techniques described herein.

These techniques are basic to all types of rifle shooting, but I apply them here with certain types of shooting in mind. The skills and techniques covered are designed for the hunter of large or small game with either centerfire or rimfire rifle, accentuating the use of field positions and taking into consideration the pressure of time, out to reasonable distances (about 300 yards). I will also touch upon ballistics and trajectory, sighting devices, the effects of wind, selection of the proper bullet, and practical accuracy requirements so that a well-rounded understanding of the intended task may be acquired, and errors in practical application avoided.

The use of the rifle in the game field by the average hunter seems to have moved rather in a backwards direction over the last generation or two. Certain techniques have been long forgotten, ignored, or have never made it into general knowledge, especially with the present tendency of so many rifle shooters to either never leave the shooting bench, or to depend entirely on bipods or shooting sticks when they do. It is my intent to bring the full blend of old and new rifle techniques together in one reference work for the aspiring rifle shootist so that these will be less likely to fall through the cracks of time as they have in the past.

The skills and techniques covered here will be useful for almost every type of shooting because they heavily emphasize the basic fundamentals of sight alignment, sight picture, trigger control, loop sling, and position. This is not a specialized tome on either target shooting competition or the use of the rifle in battle, though it borrows heavily from the former's principles of precision shooting and may provide some useful insights for the latter purpose.

These techniques have been gleaned from years of experience in both smallbore and highpower rifle bullseye competition, IPSC/USPSA practical rifle shooting competition, formal raining in hunting rifle use by Col. Jeff Cooper, much discussion with fellow competitors and students, and a select bit of reading. For rifle, they are the classic fundamentals of rifle marksmanship long recognized by position target shooters and the Marine Corps as being what works. I realize that there is more than one way to skin a cat, and some readers may have come up through a different system, but it has been my observation that all the good systems I have yet seen share the same basic fundamentals and the differences are mainly in the small details. If you have come up through an incorrect or incomplete system, or no system at all, and have an incorrect or incomplete understanding of fundamentals, then this book is for you.

I make no claim to having invented anything presented in this book; that credit belongs to the competitors and trainers who have striven and sweated and questioned over many decades. However, I may have my own slant when explaining certain aspects of the content. One of those slants is an inherent conservatism and caution which readers of the opposite tendency may find amusing. All I can say is, we are all victims of our experience, and I have had just enough to make me lean that way. Your mileage may vary. The target and the clock are always the final judges.

While there is no substitute for being trained by a proper coach, my goal here is to present this material in sufficiently clear, complete, and ordered form so that the reader can not only understand and perform these techniques, but also gain a good practice regimen to be able to improve and judge these skills, and be able to self-diagnose any problems that might arise. I want you to learn to handle your firearm safely, efficiently, quickly, and smoothly, and be able to place consistently accurate shots on your target, near or far, with the maximum amount of speed possible for your existing skill level – and to be able to continuously improve. Most importantly, I want to help you get your thinking about firearms and shooting oriented in the correct way.

Whether for the use of the rifle for quick and accurate field shooting or formal competition shooting, having the correct mindset and knowledge in your head will both prevent major mistakes and help you perform at your best.

In the interest of safety first, here are the four basic rules of gunhandling safety, per Col. Jeff Cooper:

ALL GUNS ARE ALWAYS LOADED. This does not mean you keep your guns loaded all the time. It means you always treat a gun as though it were loaded EVEN WHEN YOU KNOW IT IS NOT. The reason is that some people seem to think it is okay to handle a gun less safely if they think it is unloaded. The problem with this is that they may be mistaken! "I didn't know it was loaded!" is the cry heard after an accidental (actually, negligent) discharge, assuming the discharger is still alive. First, know how to check if any gun is loaded or unloaded; second, perform this check every time you handle a gun; third, regardless of the gun's condition, ALWAYS TREAT IT AS IF IT IS LOADED ALL THE TIME! This will cover your butt in case you are in error, and ingrain good safety habits.

NEVER LET THE MUZZLE POINT AT ANYTHING YOU DO NOT WISH TO DESTROY. Keep in control of the muzzle direction at all times and keep it in a safe direction. Know where a safe direction is.

KEEP YOUR FINGER OFF THE TRIGGER UNTIL YOUR SIGHTS ARE ON THE TARGET. The trigger fires the gun. You have no business casually placing your finger on it while handling a gun other than in the act of firing. This is probably the worst habit untrained people display; the finger goes right on the trigger as soon as they pick up the gun. Keep the finger straight along the outside of the trigger guard.

BE CERTAIN OF YOUR TARGET AND WHAT IS BEYOND IT. Do not fire at a sound or an unidentified shape. When practicing, make sure you have a safe backstop to halt every bullet you fire. Bullets tend to go through things, so even if you hit your target, the bullet can keep going. A miss keeps going too. Make sure you can control where every bullet stops.

Remember, a bullet has no friends once it leaves the gun muzzle, and you can't stop it or turn it. You are responsible for the final resting place of every bullet you shoot.

These rules must be adhered to AT ALL TIMES when handling guns, either on the range, at home, in a gun store or gun show, etc. NO EXCEPTIONS! Lives are at stake.

Keep your wits about you and your mind on what you are doing whenever you are handling a firearm. If you can't do two things at once, put the gun down, attend to whatever is distracting you, and then resume the gun business. These four rules must become second nature if you are to have anything to do with firearms. YOU are responsible every second you have a gun in your hands.

Some or all of the following information may be new to you. When going from familiar techniques to new ones, please keep in mind that you will probably do worse with the new than with the old, until you get familiar with the new. Please give the new stuff the patience and time it deserves to learn it well.

Be safe and train smart.

CHAPTER 1

WHAT ARE WE TRYING TO ACCOMPLISH?

"The purpose of shooting is hitting.
If you can get closer, get closer.
If you can get steadier, get steadier.
If you can see it, you should be able to hit it." - Col. Jeff Cooper

The purpose of this chapter is to set the direction of our thinking, and thus our training. If we set out to accomplish something, we first need to have the right idea of what that is. So, what does it mean to be a better rifle shooter? The ability to hold more steadily and hit more consistently, in less time? The ability to quickly assume a solid shooting position, either at the range or in the field, that keeps your sights on target without wobbling off your aim point? To fully know and understand all the principles and techniques of rifle marksmanship? To come up with a set of performance standards for yourself, and then develop a practice routine with which you can achieve and improve upon those standards?

The general-purpose use of a modern hunting rifle in pursuit of big game does not require quite the rarified skill sets of, say, the high power bullseye across-the-course shooter or the 1000-yard Palma competitor. However, a good understanding of and basic ability in the fundamental techniques required by these demanding disciplines goes a long way toward creating a well-rounded, competent rifle shooter who has the ability to make a quick, clean, game-killing shot at normal hunting ranges. These techniques primarily involve gun mount, sight usage, trigger management, breath control, the shooting loop sling, proper shooting position, and natural point of aim, among others. A full understanding of and capability in these skills will serve us well whether we are on the target range, in the hunting field, or in war. We would also like to know with certainty both our abilities and limitations.

We would always like to stalk our quarry as closely as possible, and use some sort of artificial rest. In reality, we may be forced to hold up and shoot further away from our quarry than we desire, and a rest may not always be available. Since position shooting without a rest requires more knowledge than shooting with a rest, and since good position skills will improve performance even with a rest, and since few people have been given proper training in posi-

Field expedient support in standing position.

tion shooting (and hence tend to rely exclusively on rests), this book will focus primarily on gaining skills in un-rested position shooting (though rests will be covered) to distances of about 300 yards, which covers the vast majority of hunting circumstances, even in the western U.S.

Our goal as hunters is to place our first shot within the heart-lung area (7-10-inch diameter) of a big game animal:
- in the minimum time possible,
- at whatever unknown distance the target presents itself (within reasonable range, which I consider to be about 300 yards),
- using the steadiest field shooting position we can apply under the circumstances,
- under the pressure of unknown time limits,
- at least nine tries out of ten.

A useful, life-sized practice target.

This is the criteria for the training format of the General Rifle class as taught by Col. Jeff Cooper at Gunsite Training Academy for many years, and it sums up the task of the rifle hunter perfectly.

When I refer to "reasonable range," I mean the furthest distance that range can be judged with acceptable accuracy by the hunter's eye, at which:
- a hit in an animal's heart-lung area can be achieved by holding no higher than on or slightly above the animal's upper back line (assuming a proper point-blank zero, discussed later),
- bullet velocity is sufficient for both penetration and expansion, and
- wind drift compensation is relatively easily made.

In other words, it's a low-complexity shot with a 90% or better chance of being a quick, clean, one-shot kill. This distance tends to be approximately 300 yards. This obviously will be well short of the cartridge's power range – but our limiting factor here is the shooter's field skill, not cartridge power. Keep that firmly in mind. And 300 yards, for the vast majority of hunters, should cover well over 90% of their hunting situations.

My justification for reasonable range is respect for the game animal. I have a prejudice against making very long shots on big game. The chances of wounding the animal with a very long shot, and then not being able to find the exact spot where it was standing in order to begin tracking it, are far too high for the vast majority of rifle shooters. A small percentage of rifle shooters are skilled enough to make hits at 350-450 yards or even further under field conditions. For most rifle-toters I have witnessed, this

Reversed kneeling over a fallen tree.

Sitting over a fallen tree, using pack to gain extra aiming height.

range limit is considerably shorter (well under 175 yards, by my observations).

While the purpose of this book is to extend the reader's practical field accuracy range, I still tend to regard 300 yards as a practical and ethical big game hunting limit for most hunters in most situations. Why? Because it fulfills the criteria in the preceding paragraph, and because as the range increases beyond 300, the variables involved (range estimation, trajectory compensation, wind reading, and wind compensation) increase the difficulty of the shot exponentially. This is important. And if you insist on taking further shots, it will be a lot easier to learn how after you first make yourself an expert field shot – getting consistently accurate and fast first-round hits – out to 300.

TASK ANALYSIS

A tight focus on the essentials will make the most constructive use of our limited training time and budget, and give us the best results. In order to create the correct training regimen, let's properly analyze our goal to derive the necessary equipment and shooter performance parameters required to meet it. Gaining a thorough understanding of all the factors involved in success is the first step. This helps us avoid error in understanding and execution. We must also understand the capabilities and limitations of our rifles, our ammunition, and ourselves.

Some counter-productive practices you might want to avoid include:

- too much time shooting from the bench in pursuit of unnecessary rifle accuracy and not enough practice from field positions (perfecting equipment rather than self);

- trying shots in excess of 300 yards while not knowing what the drop of the bullet is below the crosshair intersection, or not realizing what effect the wind might have on the bullet;
- not knowing where the rifle is zeroed;
- using a bullet design or weight that is unsuitable for the game hunted; and
- hunting dense woods with scope set to the highest magnification level, shrinking the field of view to unusable size.

Each of these can (and probably will) cause either a missed shot, a non-lethal wound to an animal, or a missed opportunity to take a shot.

All of these errors stem from misunderstanding the task at hand, either in some specific detail or as a whole. Part of my purpose here is to facilitate a fuller understanding of these matters, so you can apply this understanding to any situation you are likely to encounter, and avoid these kinds of mistakes.

The same goes for our own performance envelope. Just because we once pulled off a near-miraculous shot (perhaps by luck), doesn't necessarily mean we can do it on demand, every time, like a machine. Each of us has natural strengths and weaknesses in performing the acts required to fire an accurate shot in a short time. Honestly appraising our weaknesses allows us to define those areas in which we need to improve, and also brings us to a realistic understanding of what our own capabilities and limitations truly are. This in turn helps us to both correctly orient our training and

Taking the far shot from prone with loop sling.

make intelligent decisions about taking shots in the field.

Taking the time to select a suitably steady position instead of shooting from standing, recognizing that the wind is strong enough to require aim compensation, or realizing that a given shot is beyond our capabilities from that distance or position are all examples of using self-awareness of one's skill and knowledge levels in order to avoid missing or wounding a game animal.

We only have so much time to devote to rifle practice. Which is wiser: spending most of your range time and ammo budget trying to get your rifle to go from shooting a one-inch group at 100 yards off the bench to shooting a half-inch group, or to spend that time and money practicing position shooting? Which do you think will pay off more in the field? So, let's first get our heads in the right place about what we are trying to do, then proceed from here.

EQUIPMENT

Let's look at equipment requirements first. Besides the mechanical accuracy of the rifle/ammo combination within our desired effective range, we also have:

- the relative precision of the sighting device we use,
- flatness of bullet trajectory beyond our zeroing distance,
- bullet resistance to wind drift, and
- terminal performance of the bullet on impact.

The purpose of the discussion here is simply to create an outline of minimum requirements, we'll go into greater detail later.

MECHANICAL ACCURACY

Accuracy requirements for center-fire big game rifles vary. The kill zone of an antelope might be as small as six or seven inches, while that of an elk or moose will be ten to twelve inches or even larger. Therefore, even if our rifle/ammo combination shoots 1.5 inches at 100 yards, and say five inches at 300 yards, we can reasonably expect to land a shot in the kill zone of even an antelope at 300 yards if we do everything right. As you can see, such accuracy would suffice for any larger animal at that distance, and even further. Even a garden-variety rifle shooting six-inch groups at 300 yards will do the job on a deer or an elk inside that range – if the shooter can steadily hold correctly.

Therefore, while having a rifle that shoots sub-inch groups off the bench at 100 yards is nice and will help your confidence level in your equipment, please don't think it's at all necessary for general-purpose big-game hunting out to 300 yards. There are other and better ways to build confidence in yourself, as we shall see, and I believe that, as long as your equipment is not inferior to your task, your skill matters more than your equipment!

"But if I miss, I want to know it was me and not the rifle!" is the response I've heard a hundred times. Look at it this way: a properly-handled 1.5-inch-at-100-yards rifle will not miss a deer's kill zone (eight to nine inches) at 300 yards due to rifle inaccuracy. Improperly-handled rifles of any accuracy level have missed so many animals inside 150 yards that, if I had a dollar for each, I could retire. So, please put the above quote out of your mind for good. You matter far more

For greater steadiness, use your gear for a rest.

than the rifle; this is the proper accuracy mindset.

Example: A shooter who takes ten shots at a 10-inch target at 300 yards from an un-rested field position (no bipod, rest, or shooting sticks), with a rifle capable of a 3-4-inch group at that distance, and who only gets five or fewer hits on that target, will gain far more hits by learning better marksmanship skills than by buying a rifle that shoots a 1.5-inch group at 300 yards. If the original equipment will easily do the task, the reasons for missing are not the equipment, but the shooter, so trying to improve the equipment does nothing to solve the problem. A more accurate rifle might gain one or even two more hits in this scenario, but a properly skilled marksman can take that 3-4-inches-at-300 rifle and shoot all ten shots into a nice round 5-6-inch group dead center in the target from prone with a sling! This may make perfect sense to you, but I have run into some folks who would shake their heads and first go for that 1.5-inch rifle. For some, it's way more fun (and easier!) to buy better equipment than to work up a sweat in long sessions of position practice. Please, try to not let an obsession for perfect equipment prevent you from perfecting yourself. The purpose of perfecting yourself is to be able to shoot up to the capabilities of your rifle. In my not-so-humble opinion, to buy new, better equipment with extra, expensive capabilities you cannot even come close to applying is a waste of money which would be better spent on practice ammo with your current rifle. When you can shoot up to the capabilities of your current rifle, that is the time to upgrade.

So, as far as accuracy goes, a rifle/ammo combo that shoots no more than, say, one and a half inches at 100 yards will suffice for almost any big-game hunting within normal hunting ranges (under 300 yards). It is desirable to get your equipment combo down to one inch to one and a quarter inches at 100 yards, but even this is not strictly necessary, and any further improvements fall under the category of "accuracy for its own sake" rather than that which is necessary to accomplish this task.

Try to not let an obsession for perfect equipment prevent you from perfecting yourself.

If you insist on long-range shooting (beyond 300 yards), then of course it pays to have the most accuracy you can get. This normally tends to be more the domain of the varmint hunter, but in recent years a desire has emerged to snipe big game from extremely long ranges. This is a highly specialized pursuit requiring both a high level of skill and a high level of equipment performance, which I consider outside the domain of the general-purpose, normal-range foundational shooting skills I address here. However, the mastering of these foundational skills is the required stepping stone to those more advanced challenges.

Caveat: most people assume that group size is a straight cone with distance; that is, they assume a one-inch group at 100 yards means a two-inch group at 200 and a three-inch group at

Will your skills be sufficient at the moment of truth?

300. This is not necessarily the case. Poor quality bullets will cause groups to open up more than this the further out you shoot. And, believe it or not, some types of bullets will shoot the same groups at 300 as they do at 200, going below linear within certain yardages. Only testing at the actual ranges will tell the truth. And this testing at actual distances is necessary to both confirm your rifle's accuracy and check the bullet rise or drop from the center of the crosshairs, both closer and further than your chosen zero distance (this will be covered fully in the chapter on external ballistics).

PRECISION SIGHTING

The sighting device we use will greatly impact our ability to put our rifle's accuracy to use. Open iron sights, especially with a bead front, are a very coarse aiming tool designed for short range. Much superior to this is an aperture rear sight with a square-topped post front sight. This can allow accurate shooting throughout the normal hunting distance if your eyes are very good. Iron sights are somewhat taken for granted these days in that a lot of people do not really know the best techniques to use them, or their true potential, which I will cover. Most folks simply ignore them and mount a scope. A scope is so much superior to iron sights that almost everyone these days mounts a scope on their rifle, even on .30-30s. This is all well and fine, but there are a few points regarding scopes of which we should be aware. One is the effect of parallax. Another is learning how to use the reticle as either a range-finding or holdover-judging device. Still others are appro-

priate field of view and quick acquisition of the view. All these variables have an effect on how well we can put the rifle to use, and are covered in depth in the chapter on sights.

TRAJECTORY

Understanding trajectory allows us to shoot well beyond our zero distance. Many people do not fully understand the accelerating effects of gravity on a bullet, nor how this combines with the deceleration of bullet speed to create a radically increasing bullet drop in a very short distance beyond our zero point distance. This makes range estimation critical. Combined with a detailed knowledge of our bullet's path, it allows us to both zero correctly for our general purpose use and compensate correctly for longer shots.

WIND DRIFT

Wind drift may push the bullet sideways in its flight. Some types and weights of bullets resist the wind better than others. Learning how to judge the wind's effect on your bullet and how to compensate will be necessary if you are to hit at the longer ranges, say 250-300 yards and beyond.

TERMINAL IMPACT

Terminal impact of the bullet is what gets us the final result: a dead game animal. The bullet must hold together without disintegrating and penetrate deeply enough on raking-angle shots to get through the heart and lung area and still have some expansion. Choosing the right bullet for the task at hand can be critical, so a basic understanding of the various bullet construction types can help keep us from making a bad mistake.

KNOW THYSELF

On a personal level, we need to be able to judge several factors immediately upon sighting our quarry:

- the approximate range,
- whether this range is within our demonstrated skill level (and thus whether to shoot or not),
- what shooting position to use to make the shot (if we deem it possible), and
- whether this position is possible to assume in our location, and if not, how to stalk closer to a better location.

This requires us to be very good at shooting from different positions, as well as knowing just what we can accomplish from each position. We also need to know the biology of our quarry well enough to be able to pick out the correct aiming point to get the bullet into the heart/lung area. Once these decisions are made, the next steps are the quick assumption of a sufficiently steady proper shooting position, aim adjustments for range and wind drift if necessary, and a gentle, controlled trigger press. Accuracy is the paramount requirement, but quickness is also highly desirable, if not always necessary. Also necessary are mental and emotional self-control and tight concentration. Consider that half of your skill is going to be physical – executing a good position and firing the shot, while the other half will be mental – the development of a cool, composed, "fire-control computer" in your mind.

These are the parameters that we need to meet with both equipment and self.

Sound fundamentals are crucial for challenging shots, but add to them with every steadiness advantage you can.

Since this book is not about equipment, I will treat that in only a generalized fashion in the following chapter, sufficient to properly orient someone new to the sport, and leave you to the perusal of the many fine books and magazines about rifles and scopes. I will however touch upon ballistics, bullets, wind drift, and how best to use whatever sights you have in greater detail in later chapters.

A FEW TERMS AND CONCEPTS

Before we go any further, let me define some terms and concepts that will crop up as you read on.

When I use the term strong side or strong hand or trigger hand, I am talking about the hand that holds the pistol grip and pulls the trigger, or that side of the body (arm, leg, whatever). When I use the term support hand or support side, I am talking about the arm or hand that is holding the rifle's fore-end, or that same side of the body.

When I use the term ready position, I mean standing up with the rifle in your hands, barrel elevated and pointing up and ahead, buttstock at the strong-side hip, with the body turned slightly to the strong side as though about to take a shot from the standing position. The barrel muzzle should be in line with but just below your eyesight line, and when you scan from side to side with your eyes, you rotate your body so that the muzzle follows your gaze – "eyes, muzzle, target" as Colonel Cooper puts it. This allows instant mounting of the rifle with it already in line with any target you discover.

When I use the term dry-fire, this denotes practicing the motions of firing

100-yard smallbore target with 8-inch bull. Standing, 100 yards, using hasty-hasty Ching sling.

with an unloaded rifle up to and including the trigger press (and you really need to make sure it's empty!).

GOALS AND EXPECTATIONS

By the time you are finished with this book, and if you are reasonably physically fit and limber, you should have enough information to embark upon a training program designed to develop the following consistent skills, all without a bipod, shooting sticks, or other rest:

- Attain a shooting position that allows a steady hold that stays dead-on your target with little or no muscle tension required to either hold up the rifle or keep it aimed on target.
- Starting from standing ready, hit an 8-10-inch circle at 50 yards in 1.5 seconds from the standing position.
- Starting from standing ready, hit an 8-10-inch circle at 100 yards in about five seconds or less from the standing position.
- Starting from standing ready, hit an 8-10-inch circle at 200 yards in about 8-12 seconds from the sitting position.
- From an already-established sitting position, hit a saucer-sized (5-6-inch) target at 250 yards in under eight seconds.
- Starting from standing ready, hit an 8-10-inch circle at 300 yards in about 10-15 seconds from prone.

For an eight-inch target, the 100-yard NRA smallbore rifle target, with its eight-inch black and one-inch scoring rings, makes a good representation of a big-game animal's vital zone. If you want to save a little money, find some cheap paper plates of about the same size (most will run towards nine to ten inches). Remember that a big game animal's target area is not an exact point, but rather a zone, and while we try to aim and hit center, any hit within this zone will bring us the results we desire. If you are using a .22 rimfire within 100 yards, you can use targets of two to three inches in diameter.

Whether you attain these goals or not depends on a number of variables, not the least being how much you practice, as well as any personal physical and mental issues such as quality of vision, limberness of body, self-control, nerve damage, etc. A young healthy person in top physical shape with none of these issues should have no problem attaining the above skills with sufficient practice. The rest of us will simply do the best we can with what nature has provided us. If the above skill list sounds desirable, read on.

100-yard smallbore target. Five shots from open-leg sitting using Ching sling, at 200 yards.

SHOOTING DRILL: MEASURE YOUR CURRENT ABILITY

Before applying the techniques and training from this book, first try a simple exercise to measure your current ability level. This is the "Plate Drill" (thanks to John Schaefer of Arizona).

Take a paper plate (9-10-inch diameter) set at 100 yards and take ten shots at it, time limit two minutes. Start the drill standing with the rifle slung on your shoulder and loaded with no more than five rounds. Shoot from any position you desire, but NOT off a bench, bipod, or other rest. Use your sling if you so desire.

Run this test a couple of times and note how many times you hit the plate, the time required, group size, and the position you used. Later, after learning and practicing the techniques, you can try it again and see what improvements you've made.

CHAPTER 2

THE RIFLE AND ITS CARTRIDGE

Again, this is not a book about guns or about hunting. However, I believe it is necessary to cover a few basic points, especially for those new to the shooting sports. How we choose our rifle and cartridge, and how familiar we become with them, are very important to the results we get in the field. So rather than write a detailed buyer's guide to rifles and cartridges – there are plenty of those on the market – I will cover the matter in general, with an eye towards how we might want to think about such matters.

There are two basic ways to regard guns: either as tools to do a job or as neat toys that catch our eye. Most gun people tend to display both behaviors, depending on our mood and on what we already own. Most of us know enough to choose an appropriate tool for the job, but gun magazines lure us with the latest eye candy in the form of new guns, cartridges, scopes, etc., and those of us new to the subject may be led astray.

If we just want a new toy (and who doesn't?), fine, but keeping our eye on what we are trying to accomplish with it will help us avoid making mistakes. In "tool" terms, we need to know exactly how we are going to use our rifle before we can know what to look for in the store in terms of both rifle and cartridge selection. For the cartridge, this means first knowing how big a bullet we need

to cleanly kill our quarry. This tells us caliber requirements. Second, we need to know how our hunting terrain will dictate our range of shooting. This tells us how big a cartridge case (powder charge) we need. For the rifle size and weight, we need to know what kind of terrain we will be hunting and whether we will primarily sit or walk.

If your style of hunting is to sit and wait at a clearing a short distance from your car and your shots may be long, then a heavy rifle will be no trouble, but rather an asset. Not so if your hunting style is to hike for miles over steep, densely-wooded, rocky, rugged mountains – especially if you are getting a bit older, heavier, or are not quite in the condition you "used to was." There is something to be said for a bit of weight in the rifle to aid steadiness, but you don't want to overdo it in a carrying rifle. You can take a short, light rifle, such as Remington's Model 7, and add some lead weights in the fore-end under the barrel channel, if necessary. Plus, we will be covering ways to get quite steady in the field by proper position. Long barrels on "beanfield" rifles will get snagged on tree limbs and brush in heavy cover, especially if you are carrying it slung (which you shouldn't).

RIFLE CONSIDERATIONS

A good trigger is probably the most important aspect of any rifle, perhaps

The classic Winchester 94 lever-action carbine, in .30-30 Winchester.

Left, Remington. Model 7 bolt-action light sporter in .243. Right, custom Mauser 98 bolt-action in .35 Whelen Improved, with half-octagon barrel.

even more so than its accuracy potential, since it is the interface between the shooter and the shot. A heavy, creepy, gritty trigger is the enemy of an accurate shot. This is supremely important. Any rifle you own should have a trigger pull that is, or can be made, crisp (no apparent movement or creep while being pulled) and set at about two and a half to three and a half pounds of pull weight.

Whatever action type you choose, become intimately familiar with its workings. Learn to work the action with the

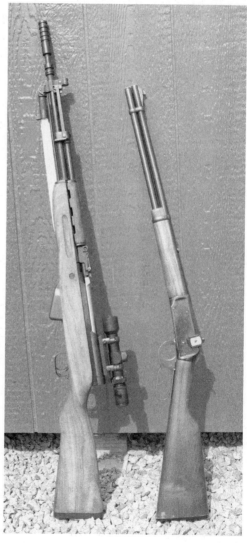

AR-15 semi-autoVarminter in .223.

Left to right: Scoped SKS semi-auto in 7.63x39 mm, Winchester 94 lever-action in .30-30.

rifle at your shoulder in firing position. Learn to reload it by feel, without having to look at the rifle, so you can keep your eyes on your target. Practice mounting the gun to the shoulder, as described in a later chapter, so that the sights automatically align with your target. When you step into the woods on the first day of the season, your rifle should not feel unfamiliar in your hands.

Generally speaking, bolt actions and single shots will be the most accurate, with pump and lever guns being quite a bit less so. Some of the autoloading ri-

Left to right: Marlin 795 .22 rimfire semi-auto, Remington 541-S .22 rimfire bolt-action, Remington 540-X .22 rimfire bolt-action target rifle, customized Ruger 10-22 .22 rimfire semi-auto, standard Ruger 10-22.

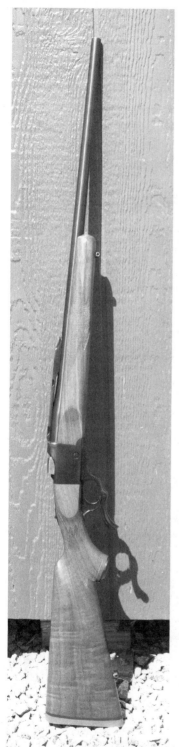

Ruger No. 1 single-shot in .280 Remington.

It's helpful to know the difference between what you desire and what you need.

fles, such as the Browning Automatic Rifle, have a reputation for good accuracy, while most others are about on par with pump and lever actions. Again, remember that even the unimpressive 3-inch-at-100-yards accuracy of a tired old Winchester 94 or Savage 99 lever gun will do fine for killing a deer at 150 yards in the timber. You may lust after the half-inch-at-100 rifle, and that's fine. Remember that it's helpful to know the difference between what you desire and what you need.

CARTRIDGE CONSIDERATIONS

Ditto with cartridges. You don't need the .300 Remington Ultra Mag to hunt deer in the forest (there is a reason the old .30-30 is still highly popular, after all). When it comes to a first-shot hit on an animal's kill zone at unknown distance from a field position, most rifle shooters are nowhere near up to the range capability of their cartridges. If you consider that the vast majority of game animals are probably shot within 200 yards, and probably most of these under 150 yards, it follows that old-fashioned, standard cartridges like the .30-30, .243, .308, .270, and .30-06 will work just fine for almost any situation. New and sexy? Nope, sorry. Highly effective, economical, and easy on the shoulder? Yep.

Big magnum ammunition is not only expensive to buy, but it is hard on your shoulder too. If shooting your rifle is unpleasant, you won't spend any range time with it, and it will make you flinch, a

Left to right: Remington Model 7 .243 bolt-action, AR-15 Varminter, scoped M1 carbine semi-auto.

bad habit and one that's tough to break. Ideally you want a cartridge that you can shoot at least 40 times per practice session without discomfort or developing a flinch. It should be economical enough that you can do this at least once a month, every month, without busting your budget. Finally, it should deliver enough power to cleanly kill your quarry at the distance and in the terrain you typically hunt, and that your skill level will allow.

Rather than go into the whole range of cartridges available, I will touch upon the general groupings by power class.

There are currently several different classes of cartridges for big game. The old standby .30-06 and its descendants based on that case (.25-06, .270, .280,

Left to right: Mauser 98 bolt-action sporter in .35 Whelen Improved, scoped SKS semi-auto, Enfield No. 4 .303 bolt-action with a USGI M1907 sling, Savage 99 lever-action in .308 Win., Winchester 94 lever-action carbine in .30-30 Win.

.35 Whelen, and the wildcats 6.5mm-06, 8mm-06, and .338-06) are "standard length" cartridges. The power developed in this case size will top well over 3000 feet per second velocity in the smaller calibers with the lighter bullets, and allow fairly flat shooting and good killing power on antelope and deer past 300 yards.

The .30-06 edges up into elk and moose category with velocities ranging from 2400 fps with the 220 grain bullet up to 2900 fps with the 150 grain, and perhaps the same range.

The .35 Whelen delivers about 2600 fps velocity with the mid-weight 225 grain bullet, which just about makes it to 300 without an inordinate amount of drop.

If you want to hunt game no bigger than deer, and expect shots to be a little on the longish side, the .25-06 and .270 are as big as you need to go. If elk is on the menu, then the .280 might be considered the minimum desirable. Yes, people have killed loads of elk with the .270, and I hunt elk with it myself. But I consider it marginal. I only use it because I load the heaviest available bullets of the stoutest construction (150/160 Nosler Partition or 150 Barnes X) and I know I have the skill level to make a careful shot, the self-knowledge to know what my limitations are, and the will power to say no to a shot I think is beyond those limitations. If you are going to go light in cartridge for a given animal, you need to be able to do the same.

The short-action class of cartridges originated way back with the .30-30, .303 Savage, .250 Savage (parent of the

The 7.62x39 mm, left, and the .30-30 Winchester. The former, with proper hunting bullet, will take deer at closer ranges.

Left to right - .22LR, 6mm Tejas (modified 6BR Remington), .243 Winchester, .223 Remington.

much more well-known .22-250) and the .300 Savage (parent case of the .308). Most of these rounds are almost forgotten today, and have been displaced by the well-known .308 and its descendants. These cartridges (.243, .260, 7mm-08, .308, .358, and the new .338 Federal) essentially parallel the standard-length cartridges but at a reduced power level, due to the case length being about ½-inch shorter. Figure that velocities will run about 125-160 fps less in a short-action round versus a standard-length round of the same caliber and bullet weight. This results in slightly less usable range, though in the field it will be hard to tell the difference with equal bullet weights.

Where the short-action cartridges lose out to the standard-length rounds is in the ability to handle the heaviest bullet weights for that caliber. Often, factory loads are not available in short-action cartridges using the heaviest bullet available in factory loads for the equal-caliber standard-length round. For example, the .30-06 can be had with 220 grain bullets, but the .308 tops out at 200 grains. The 7mm-08 is most often found with 120 and 140 grain bullets, yet the .280 Remington can be had in 160 and 175 grain bullets. The reduced powder capacity of the short-action cases prevents the use of heavy-for-caliber bullets.

These cartridges have moderate to light recoil, are very accurate, and are excellent choices for hunting animals from

The .308 Winchester, .303 British, .30-06, .375 H&H Magnum, 8mm Remington Magnum, .270 Winchester, and .45-70.

antelope up to large deer at ranges out to 275-300 yards, in skilled hands. The .308, .338 Federal, and .358 are suitable for larger animals like elk and black bear at similar ranges, perhaps a bit shorter with the .358. The 7mm-08 is marginal for the larger animals, but will probably do fine if the hunter uses a stoutly-constructed heavy bullet (160 grains), limits range to about 250 yards, and places it with precision.

The smaller calibers lack both velocity and bullet weight to be considered optimum for elk and larger animals. They certainly will kill, and you may know someone who successfully hunts elk with a .243. But, they are not the best tools for the job, especially if you don't want to have to track a fatally-wounded runner down into a steep thickly-brushed canyon. If you want a short-action, non-magnum, do-everything cartridge, you can't beat the .308.

MAGNUM CARTRIDGES

The standard-length magnum cartridges (.264 Winchester Magnum, 7 millimeter Remington Magnum, .300 Winchester Magnum, .338 Winchester Magnum) by contrast boost velocities about 200-300 fps more than a standard-length round and offer a flatter trajectory over a longer distance. This may add perhaps another 100-150 yards of usable range, due mostly to the ability to zero the rifle another 50 or so yards further out than the usual 200 yards. The case diameter is quite a bit larger than that of the .30-06.

The price for this performance gain is increased blast, recoil, and cost. They are best used for applications where the

shooting distance is expected to consistently be more than 200 yards and probably beyond 300, and/or where a heavy-for-caliber bullet or large-caliber bullet at high velocity is deemed necessary to either defeat the wind at distance or to really put a slam on a tough animal that, taking exception to being shot, might amble over and tear your impertinent head off.

Recently there have been introduced the short-action magnum rounds, the super-short magnum rounds, and huge ultra-magnum rounds. The first offer nearly standard-length magnum performance from short-action rifles and are something to seriously consider if you feel you need great power in a small package. The second have very short and very fat cases, which theoretically boost cartridge efficiency. The last are the approximation of a Saturn V moon rocket booster in the cartridge world, hurling medium (7mm, .30, .338) caliber bullets at astonishing velocities for very long range shooting.

One thing to keep in mind with any magnum, besides extra cost, blast, and recoil, is the fact that the more powder you burn down a given bore diameter the quicker you will burn out that critical area of the barrel just ahead of the chamber where the rifling grooves begin. This area is called the throat, and once it begins to erode from the heat of firing, your accuracy goes downhill quickly.

With the small-caliber magnums, accurate barrel life can be as little as 1000-1200 rounds before rapid degeneration starts. This is true even of some non-magnum rounds like the .22-250 and

.243. So, if you like to shoot a lot, keep this in mind when selecting a cartridge. While most rifle hunters only shoot a few boxes of shells a year (or even less), some of us like to shoot a whole lot more. Shooting from 200 to 400 centerfire rounds a year through a properly-structured training program should be a realistic goal, and 600 rounds should not be out of the question. Of course, using a .22 rimfire rifle of the same configuration as your primary centerfire rifle is an enormous help, as is having a similar centerfire rifle in a caliber that is smaller, cheaper, and less throat-burning and shoulder-thumping than that .300 magnum you just had to have. If you have the disposable income, obtaining a rifle identical to your primary hunting piece but in .223 caliber makes for a very nice training piece.

HOW TO CHOOSE

In choosing from the above categories, it's important to understand whether you need more bullet or more velocity. The magnum cartridges seduce with their high velocity numbers, but think about it: a 180 grain .30 bullet is still a 180 grain .30 bullet whether fired from a .308 or a .300 Winchester Magnum. The first question that should be answered by the aspiring rifle hunter is, "how big a bullet do I need?" Then the question of velocity is answered by how far you think you need to shoot that bullet. Remember that speed and muzzle energy (which is highly dependent upon speed) disappears with distance, but a bullet's mass and diameter remain constant. Start your considerations with bullet diameter and weight.

As you can see, a short-action cartridge from .243 to .358 will handle the vast majority of deer hunting requirements within normal hunting ranges, and without breaking either your shoulder or your wallet. For shooting at larger game and/or using heavy-for-caliber bullets, and gaining just a smidgen more range, the standard-length .30-06-based rounds are hard to beat, though there is a slightly more noticeable level of recoil. The magnums are generally overkill for hunting under 300 yards. The .25-06, .270, .280, and .30-06 will do anything you need done at these ranges, if you use the right bullet and place it in the right spot. And 300 yards is a long, long way. As the old saying goes, "If you can't do it with a .30-06, you probably shouldn't even be trying." Where magnums shine, though, is shooting a heavy bullet somewhat flatter at longer ranges and with shorter flight time.

And this last bit, shorter flight time, brings up a special consideration – wind. If you live in an area where the terrain is wide open and windy, and where stalking close to game is difficult if not impossible due to lack of cover and flatness of ground, you may want to consider a cartridge that is somewhat more powerful than what you would otherwise pick for pure game-killing power. The reason is that the wind can be a difficult challenge to surmount at ranges past 300 yards. While having a relatively flat trajectory is nice, you still have to judge the range correctly and compensate for drop accordingly, whether you are shooting a 7mm magnum or a .45-70. The distance to target is fixed in either case, and the process is the same. Yet with the wind, both its

The well-dressed Rem. Model 7. Camo tape, Ching sling, cartridge cuff, and...

...cartridge ballistic information taped to stock. All ready for a hunt.

speed and direction can vary constantly, and can even have several differences in each aspect simultaneously along the line between the shooter and the target. It is a true variable, which means you cannot achieve a perfect solution since you cannot know what the exact condition of wind will be at the instant of the shot. As a result there is a fairly small margin of error inherent in correcting for wind.

Aside from becoming skilled wind readers (discussed in its own chapter later on), we can best deal with this variable by widening this margin: using a cartridge whose velocity and bullet mass are greater (and also choosing a more sleek bullet), thus offering greater resistance to wind drift, than what we might otherwise use for the game hunted. For example, while a 7mm-08 with a 140-grain bullet may be about perfect for deer under 300 yards under low-wind conditions, changing the conditions to high and variable winds and ranges of 300-400 yards would favor at least a .280 with 160-175 grain bullets or a .30-06 with 165s or 180s, and preferably some flavor of either 7mm or .300 magnum with 175s or 180s. The deer doesn't take any more killing, but the wind needs more bucking.

CHAPTER 3

THE MIND OF THE RIFLE SHOOTER

Buck fever? What's that? Die, Bambi!

This book is about human performance. The controlling characteristic of this is one's mind. Within the context of rifle shooting, there are definite ways in which our state of mind can either help or hurt us. So, it pays to recognize what to seek and what to avoid. Further, an unfortunate aspect of the human mind (especially the male mind) is the "I don't need to ask for directions/read the instructions/learn from someone else" mindset.

Now if you are reading this you probably aren't one of that crew, but it is still sometimes difficult to open our minds to new ideas or to take an honest, critical look at ourselves. However, this willingness to learn and to honestly analyze and critique one's self is an absolute requirement for progress, so try to keep that in mind whenever you start a practice session. Ego is the most self-destructive characteristic we possess; don't take it to a practice session.

There are two distinct states of mind that are important to this discussion: that which we carry around with us all the time as a normal state, and that which we experience in the "moment of truth" when we put the crosshairs on perhaps a record trophy animal. The former has a definite effect upon the latter, and the latter has a definite effect on our performance ability (ever hear of "buck fever"?). So, let's start with our normal state of mind as it applies to our view of ourselves as rifle hunters.

First, we need to have our minds right about what we are doing, as related in Chapter 1. This means having taken the time to figure out what we are trying to do and then find the best way to do it.

This in turn gives us a structured training program. What we desire to achieve here is the attitude that "if I can see it, I can hit it." This attitude comes from confidence, and confidence comes from demonstrated ability. This ability is gained and demonstrated in training – if our training mirrors what we must do in the field.

When the moment to shoot arrives in the field, what we want is mental performance that is smooth, unflustered, quick, clear, and emotionless. Yet, we are beset by a number of variables. One is the excitement of spotting our quarry. Another is the sudden need to act quickly, before the animal takes a step and vanishes. Still another is fear of failure. Range estimation, wind estimation, aim point, and appropriate shooting position must all be figured out in a hurry. If we are not used to doing these things under time pressure, at various distances and with differing target sizes, we can be a bit overwhelmed. Mistakes are likely in this condition. We realize this, and nervous anxiety increases, which can make us physically tremble, and be less than clear in our decision making.

The antidote for this is to relax and clear the mind of every consideration except those required to fire a good hit, and to have those considerations honed into our minds and bodies so that we can perform them without conscious thought. We must act like a cold, unemotional shooting machine. This is not natural for us, especially under the typical hunting circumstance, but we can train ourselves to do so – if we instill this requirement in our training program. Concentration must be total, focus must be absolute. Let your training take over. Get in the

The X-ring is three inches in diameter and 200 yards away. Concentrate!

Can you maintain your mental concentration and visual focus?

"bubble." Coolness and self-control are what enable delivery of the performance we require. If you do not have much self-control, well then, this is your chance to develop some. Without it, you will never be more than a mediocre shot.

In training, your mindset should be one of seriousness and total focus on the task at hand. Each training session should be focused on developing a certain set of skills, so that you can put your time into producing a noticeable increase in those skills by the end of each session. Be jealous of your good shots and unforgiving of misses. Train with the determination that "I WILL hit with THIS shot" every shot. If the recoil of your main rifle bothers you, wear a shoulder pad available for such purposes, get a muzzle brake on your rifle, or, best of all, just learn to ignore it. Do not rush, and do not try to force a shot that doesn't seem to want to happen. Stop, take a breath, and start over instead.

Don't try to make a shot happen, just let it happen. Relax your mind, calm yourself, and proceed with calm deliberation. Shooting a rifle is very much the opposite of many other sports activities, in that instead of trying hard to do something, you must not try hard. The more you do, the more you potentially create error. Maximum possible relaxation of mind and body bring the best results. Detach yourself from the moment, as though you were simply looking over someone else's shoulder and watching him shoot. Rifle shooting, properly understood, is a very minimalist and passive activity. Remember this when learning your positions and trigger management. Also, learn to be patient, with each shot (especially trigger

action, described later) as well as with the whole learning process.

Part of this practice is developing a level of concentration that excludes all considerations or distractions other than the factors required to fire an accurate shot. First you will decide whether or not to shoot, then which shooting position to assume for sufficient steadiness. Then you will focus on making your chosen position as perfect as possible in terms of steadiness and proper natural point of aim, in as short a time as possible. Then you will focus on aiming: sight alignment and sight picture. Then the gentle press on the trigger, in proper synchronization with your breathing cycle, for a surprise break in a compressed time period while focusing both eye and mind on your sight picture, to the total exclusion of all else except possibly a nearby nuclear explosion. Then, follow through by calling your shot by seeing where the front sight or crosshairs were at the instant of firing, seeing your sight lift in recoil so you know you didn't blink at the shot, maintaining focus on the sight picture through the recoil cycle (don't just lower the rifle and look downrange!), and seeing to where the sight recovered after recoil ends, while reflexively working the action. No other thoughts, worries, etc., allowed. You may have heard sports figures mention the terms "getting in the zone" or "getting in my bubble." This is exactly what you need to learn to do with your aiming and trigger management. It will take some time to develop, but once you get there you will know it, and it will greatly improve your performance.

Think about what you are doing. Analyze everything you do, patiently and carefully.

Experiment. If something is giving you difficulty, use the tips related in the chapter on how to practice to figure out what is going wrong. Training is a process of continuous learning and improvement, not just making noise. Put your mind to work!

The end result of this training is total knowledge of our abilities and limitations, and therefore confidence when the moment of truth arrives. This helps alleviate the sort of nervous anxiety that disrupts our steady hold and produces faulty decisions, and provides us with the Holy Grail we seek: the confident, assertive, yet judicious mindset of a skilled rifle shooter.

So how do we accomplish this? First, we master the physical fundamentals of rifle shooting, and prove to ourselves that we can deliver a bullet where we want it to go, every time. Then, we practice and test these skills in various ways, adding the pressure of time limits and friendly competition. There are drills (covered later in this work) we can perform against the clock to compete against ourselves or our shooting friends. Finally, there is formal competition, such as smallbore or highpower rifle target shooting, metallic silhouette shooting, practical 3-gun matches, and other official sports where we can test our mettle.

Competition, even against a clock, induces mental stresses absent in a more mundane trip to the range. Learning to deal with these stresses in training and competition (informal or otherwise) will not only markedly reduce them in the field, it will give you a set of well-honed responses to any situation you are likely to encounter.

The only way to eliminate stress as a performance degrader is to put yourself into a stressful situation and then focus on performing the basic fundamentals while tuning out all else – over and over and over again. If you do not think you will get a case of the jitters from someone holding a shot timer clock over your shoulder, or competing man-against-man with your shooting buddy on a steel plate target, just wait until you try it! Such informal competitive practice is a relatively gentle way of easing yourself into the notion of more formal competition, since only your buddy is watching you. Once you get used to the added pressure, and see that you can actually shoot accurately and quickly under stress, it boosts your confidence enormously, often enough to overcome the frequent "formal competition shyness" that a lot of people have. This process will provide a higher return for your efforts than you can imagine. This is very important to consider.

Once you learn the fundamentals of aiming, trigger management, and position, try to include in your training such things as targets at unknown distances, comparing two separate but close positions (squatting vs. kneeling, kneeling vs. sitting, etc.) on a target at the same distance, and those sorts of things that help your decision-making process as well as your pure marksmanship.

When in the field, keep Col. Cooper's dictum in mind at all times: "If you can get closer, get closer. If you can get steadier, get steadier." This will help you to put yourself in the best possible position for a clean one-shot kill. Work this

You might need a quick follow-up shot. Keep the rifle shouldered and your head in the game until the game goes down!

The standing ready position: eyes, muzzle, target, all in line. But are you mentally and emotionally ready?

into your training if you are able. You may want access to a large chunk of public or private land where you can not only shoot safely, but set up targets at various distances and practice a stalk.

Remember, the more comprehensive your training, the less mental work you will have to do when the game shot presents itself in the woods. The less work you have to do, the less pressure you will feel, the fewer mistakes you will make, and the faster your reaction will be.

Make part of your training the development of a "rifleshooter's mindset" that can quickly make correct decisions as to range, wind, aimpoint, best workable shooting position, and whether or not the shot is within your known capability. Do this while maintaining your cool, creating a bubble of concentration, and exercising sound judgement. This "mental fire-control computer," combined with the physical ability to get into a good, steady shooting position quickly, will allow you to hit anything you can see within reasonable ranges in literally a matter of a few seconds. That is a nice package to be able to carry with you into the woods, or on patrol in hostile territory.

Three last, rather esoteric, but important points to ponder at your leisure: First, enjoy your rifle. Take pleasure in its form and function, its heft and balance, its precision engineering and

"Target spotted - GO!"

Beautiful wood is easy to appreciate.

manufacture, and its example of artistic craftsmanship. It should make you smile when you handle it. Those of you who are professional soldiers, serious martial artists, or have a serious interest in weaponry of any kind (even your bolt-action hunting rifle is directly descended from the Mauser 98 military rifle) will know what I mean when I say that handling a good rifle should bring a warm glow of

So is a nicely-executed cheekpiece.

I love walnut that looks good enough to eat!

Yes, I can keep them out of fix-bayonet range.

pleasure. And if you are in the military or security or law enforcement, it should also give you a surge of self-confidence. Second, remember ancient Greek mythology, with Zeus, king of all the Greek gods and goddesses, standing at the top of Mt. Olympus? When someone or something down below displeased him, he could hurl thunder-and-lightning bolts down from Olympus to annihilate the target of his wrath. Your rifle, my friends, is the thunderbolt of Zeus. It gives you a superhuman power, once attributable only to the gods of old, to destroy with great power and precision at a great distance.

Like all power, this can be a fascinating and intoxicating thing. A good rifle, in the hands of a really skilled shooter, allows such a person to dominate his or her environment to a radius well beyond a quarter mile, and perhaps much further. This confidence will give you a real warm fuzzy! As noted above, if you ever have to grab a rifle in a military or civil conflict or emergency, its heft in your hands, combined with confidence in your hard-earned skills, should calm your fears and steady your mind. Its use for good or ill is entirely dependent upon the moral stature of those who wield it. As such, its employment should be considered an opportunity for the development and exercise of personal self-discipline,

responsibility, and sound judgment. This is not a small point.

Third, aside from the topic of hunting, our ancestors thought enough of your freedom to guarantee your possession of personal arms in order to defend that freedom, for yourselves and your descendants. Your rifle empowers you to do this (as a last ditch defense of course) far more effectively than any other means that will be at your disposal should straits become that dire. As the saying goes, "A man with a rifle is a citizen, a man without a rifle is a subject." In his works To Ride, Shoot Straight, and Speak the Truth and The Art of the Rifle, Col. Jeff Cooper expounds upon all this at somewhat more depth than I have here; I highly advise acquiring (not just borrowing) and reading these books. This may seem out of place in a book about learning to shoot the rifle for the purpose of hunting, but it speaks to the heart and soul of the rifle and its true meaning and potential for its owner. If you do not appreciate this, you will be missing out on what I think is probably the most important aspect of being a rifle owner. If you have not done some thinking along these lines already, this is worth serious reflection. Your reward may be a satisfaction, pride, and peace of mind that greatly enhances your joy in shooting – and living.

CHAPTER 4

SIGHTS AND AIMING

EYES

The first step in aiming is to determine whether you are right-eye or left-eye dominant. Quite a few people have never given the matter much thought, but there are a number of people whose dominant eye is not on the same side as their dominant hand. If you are cross-dominant (right-handed and left-eyed, or vice-versa) you will have to determine whether you have to shoot to your dominant eye or to your dominant hand. This is important because the brain tends to operate primarily off the perspective of one eye, and trying to aim with the weak eye may drive you nuts.

There are two basic ways to determine your dominant eye. One is to look at a distant object with both eyes open and extend your arm out with your thumb aligned with the object. Looking your thumb, first close your left eye, then open it and close your right eye. Whichever eye sees your thumb stay aligned with the object, while the other eye is closed, is your dominant eye. Whichever eye sees your thumb appear to jump sideways a bit when the other eye is closed is your non-dominant eye. The other way to check is to look at a distant object, extend your arm out to it and circle it with your thumb and forefinger, so that you are looking at the object through the circle. Then, with your focus remaining on the object, slowly bring the finger circle back

to your face. You will naturally bring it back to your dominant eye.

Most people have to aim a rifle with their dominant eye. You will probably not be able to place your face against the stock in such a way as to bring the opposite side eye behind the sights. So, if you are cross-dominant, you may have to learn to shoot with your weak-hand side. Or, you may be able to shoot with the strong-hand side if you can either close or squint your dominant eye. Closing one eye tends to produce a strain on the other one, but see if the squint method works for you. Cross-dominance is a problem that can be solved, but people will have to work out the best method for themselves.

Even if you find you can aim with your dominant eye, you still may have some issues with the non-dominant eye. Some folks just can't aim, especially through a scope, while keeping the non-aiming eye open – the brain sees conflicting optical signals. You might find you have to close the weak eye in order to concentrate on aiming. This is not necessarily a bad thing, but it cuts down on your peripheral awareness at that moment. This may put you at a disadvantage while hunting, or downright in danger in a battle. I find myself wanting to close my weak eye (as in some of the pictures) but usually I try to squint it to reduce its feed to my brain, while still

Proper offhand mount with head erect, and cheek weld giving proper eye position.

retaining some peripheral vision input. The more situational awareness you can maintain, the better.

THE MOUNT & CHEEK WELD

In order to see your sights properly, the gun must be mounted correctly to the shoulder. What makes the mount correct is the presentation of the sights directly in front of your eye, with the rifle pointed at your desired target, so that if you are looking at your target while you mount your rifle, you will have your iron sights or scope crosshairs appear superimposed on your target as the butt makes contact with your shoulder and the stock touches your cheek.

If you have ever heard someone say, "I just can't see through a scope," or seen someone shoulder a rifle then hunch their head down to get their eye behind the scope, then wave the rifle all over searching for their target, these problems are usually attributable to a faulty mount.

When mounting the rifle to your shoulder, try to bring the scope or sights into your sight line to the target and stock up to your cheek, with your head held erect, before placing the butt in your shoulder. This will eliminate a hunched-down head and place your eye behind the sights more comfortably and consistently, giving you a quicker alignment of iron sights or faster correct view through a scope. Concentrate on placing the sights or scope directly in your line of sight, while your eye is looking at the target. This will solve the problem of not being able to see through the scope right away.

By using this rifle-sights-to-eyesight-line index, rather than a butt-to-shoulder index followed by moving your eye to a position behind the sights, you will go from seeing the target with your naked eye to seeing the target through the scope or sights immediately. You are essentially guiding your gun mount position by inserting the sight into your eyesight line, rather than just bringing the butt to your shoulder.

Once you learn to mount the rifle to make this happen, make sure your face contacts the stock (the "cheek weld") in the same place in the same way every time you mount the gun, every shot. The correct and repeatable cheek weld is what guarantees proper eye alignment behind your sights. Use the visual index of seeing your sights first as you raise the rifle, in order to learn the correct physical index of where the butt goes into your shoulder and where the stock comb touches your cheek. As we will see later, a correct mount executed at high speed is instrumental in the performance of the snap shot. Perfecting this motion and making it exactly the same for each performance is absolutely critical. This is worthy of considerable practice time!

Keep your trigger-hand arm high at the elbow when in standing or kneeling position, with the arm horizontal if possible. This will form the "pocket" in your shoulder for the buttstock. This pocket is close to your neck, rather than way out on your upper arm. If you're placing the butt on the deltoid muscle – the bump at the top front of your arm – move the butt closer to your neck. Raising your strong-side arm to horizontal accentuates the difference between the pocket and the bump. Try to keep the butt in the pocket in all shooting positions whenever possible.

MINUTES OF ANGLE (MOA)

This concept is of supreme importance to the rifle shooter. It deals with how your line of aiming is related to the line of direction in which your barrel is pointed, which should be nearly parallel lines with only a tiny angle of vertical divergence. It is also how sight adjustments work to change this angular relationship so that we may achieve a proper impact of our bullet on target at a given distance (getting "zeroed"), and adjust for excessive bullet drop at long range, and for excessive wind drifting. It is a measurement of angle, with which we are all familiar (360 degrees in a circle, right?). To be expert with the rifle requires a comfortable understanding of this concept.

When your shot impacts in a different place than where you aimed, it is because your scope or sights are looking along a different line than where your barrel is pointed. This represents an angular divergence. So, to move our sights into coincidence with where the barrel sent the bullet, we need to reduce that angle to near zero so our sights are aiming right where the barrel throws the bullet. We do this by adjusting and moving our sights (usually the rear) in angular increments. Physically we rotate a knob on our scopes or peep sights, which may or may not "click" in given increments of angular rotation, and note a scale of movement which represents angular increments of sight movement. Sights are designed and (sometimes) labeled to work in whole or fractions of minutes of angle; this is why you need to understand this concept in order to use your sights accurately and efficiently.

Also, you can look at your group sizes as cones of dispersion which are measurable as an angle.

So, what does only one degree of angle spread over say, 100 yards? Just over five feet!

Well, we can hardly use that to move our group three inches at 100 yards, can we? Nope, we need something smaller. As it happens, the official subdivision of a single degree of angle is one-sixtieth of one degree, called a minute of angle. By happy fate, this equates to almost exactly one inch width at 100 yards. Now this we can use!

Besides getting a zero, if you are planning on shooting far enough to require correction in aim for either wind or trajectory, it will be useful to do your thinking about adjustments in minutes of angle. The exact width of divergence of one moa is 1.047 inches at 100 yards, 2.094 inches at 200 yards, 3.141 inches at 300 yards, 10.47 inches at 1000, and so on. For short-range shooting purposes we round it to the nearest inch, and simply remember that it is an inch for every hundred yards of distance. One moa spreads two inches at 200 yards, 3.5 inches at 350 yards, 7.25 inches at 725 yards, etc. Just take the target distance in yards, move the decimal point two places left, and that tells how many inches one moa covers at this distance. This is the "magic rule" conversion factor that allows us to convert inches on the target to moa, at any target distance. What this allows us to do is make sight adjustments very easily based on what the target shows us. Memorize the magic rule!

For example, let's say we are shooting a cartridge in a rifle zeroed dead on at

200 yards, and our ballistic information tells us that with this zero our bullet will be nine inches low at 300 yards. At this distance one minute of angle (rounded) comprises roughly three inches. Three inches (one MOA) goes into nine inches three times, so this amount of drop is three minutes of angle, or three MOA. When we look at our sights and see that they say they have adjustments of ¼ inch at 100 yards or ¼ MOA, we understand that it takes four clicks to get one minute of adjustment. So, if we want to hold dead on at 300 yards, we come up 12 clicks (our three minute of angle drop). This works equally well for horizontal adjustments to compensate for wind.

Keep in mind, however, that as distance increases past about 300 yards, that .047 inch we rounded off can start accumulating enough to make a big difference on small targets very far away. If you have to adjust your sights up four minutes of angle to use a dead-on aim at 400 yards, for example, using a true minute of angle means using 4.188 inches instead of four. Multiplying this by four will create a difference of just over 3/4 inch. Not very much, of course, but the difference gets larger the further out you go. Perfectionists and long-range shooters will let you know the error of your ways if you let them catch you rounding.

For small amounts of compensation, we can simply hold off, if the size of our target allows for accurate judging of just how much we are holding off. For example, if we are aiming at a standing woodchuck about 12 inches tall and five inches wide, it is easy to judge four or five inches of sideways hold-off and five or six inches of holdover. However, for compensation of 10 or 12 inches or more, it becomes difficult to determine just how much we actually are holding off. In reality, it becomes just a guess. Much better is to use the mechanical adjustments of the scope, which should (in quality examples) be both precise and repeatable.

Learning to think, and especially to see, in minutes of angle will help you solve aiming problems much more quickly and easily than otherwise. It is also a wise idea to categorize your accuracy capability in each shooting position by its size in minutes of angle. This provides a consistent measurement of your skill (the angular size of your group dispersion) at any distance: i.e., shooting a two inch group from sitting at 100 yards (two rounded moa) is the same accuracy and skill level as shooting an eight inch group at 400 yards (two rounded moa again).

SIGHT ALIGNMENT: IRON SIGHTS

The main thing to remember when using iron sights with any firearm is to focus on the front sight – not the target or rear sight. Let the target blur slightly in relation to the sight, as this will not hurt your aim. If the front sight is not sharply in focus, your aim will definitely suffer.

The reason you focus on the front sight is that if the target is blurry, the possible aim error from trying to hold the tip of the front sight against the blurry edge of the target will only be as big as the blurred edge appears – a quite small distance actually. But, if the front sight is blurry, you will not notice small misalignments of the sight, which, due to the angle differences between where your eye is looking and where the sights/barrel are looking, translate into enormous errors at the target. Where the front sight goes, so goes the shot. If you don't know exactly where your front sight is, you can't properly aim. Your eye can only focus at one distance at once, so make it count. The front sight is your best friend. This is of supreme importance. If you shoot with iron sights you must ingrain the reflexive habit of locking your eye focus onto the front sight the instant it enters your line of vision

Open iron sights

These are typified by a round brass bead front sight, and a leaf rear sight with a U-shaped notch cut into its concave-curved top edge (known as a "semi-buckhorn" rear sight). This is a very coarse aiming device, mostly due to the size of the bead. Most such beads will obscure eight to ten inches at 100 yards. This is fine for a deer in close timber; just cover the deer's shoulder with the bead. For finer aiming, it is at a distinct

disadvantage. The bead covers too much, and if you try to use the round top of the bead, you'll find it is somewhat more difficult to use as an aiming index than a square-top post.

The method of sight alignment with a front bead is to set the bead into the notch of the rear sight. How high or low to place it, and whether one indexes the bottom of the bead against the bottom of the notch or the top of the bead against the top of the rear sight blade, seems to be a matter of personal preference. This can cause problems when one person attempts to use a rifle so equipped that has been zeroed by someone else with a different idea of how to align the sights.

Much better is a square-topped front post sight in conjunction with a flat-topped rear blade with a square or rectangular notch. The horizontal top surface of the post is the aiming index. It is much more precise than a bead, and you can see more target over the top of it. The alignment index here is to line up the top of the front post with the top of the rear

Iron front bead sight.

Iron rear semi-buckhorn open sight.

Factory open iron sight alignment. In this view the top of the front bead is even with the top of the central portion of the rear blade, and centered from side to side in the rear notch. Note the front sight bead is sharply focused, while the rear sight is blurry. Focus on the front bead.

side in the rear sight notch. This is the same arrangement as the standard "Partridge" style set of handgun sights.

The method of focusing on metallic sights is to always focus on the front sight. With a bead you look at the face of the bead; with a post you look at its top flat surface. Your eye can only focus on one thing at a time, so don't even try to hold the rear sight, front sight, and target in focus all at once; it's impossible. The front sight is the most important, because where it goes, the shot goes.

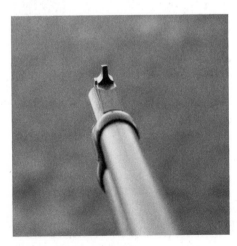

Front iron Partridge post sight.

Aperture iron sights

Aperture or "peep" sights are generally considered a huge improvement over open sights due to the rear sight being "looked through" rather than "looked at." The view through a large peep sight hole (as befits a hunting or military rifle, as opposed to the small ones used for target shooting) allows a large view of the front sight and target unobstructed by the blade of an open rear sight. This is a very accurate and fast combination, much more so than open sights. There are, however, certain things that must be known to use a peep sight properly.

Shooting aperture sights correctly requires knowledge of certain techniques. Unlike open sights, there is no specific reference point on the metal of the rear sight with which you align the front sight. Rather, you are looking through a hole, focusing on the front sight. The front sight (tip of the post or face of the

FOCUS HERE

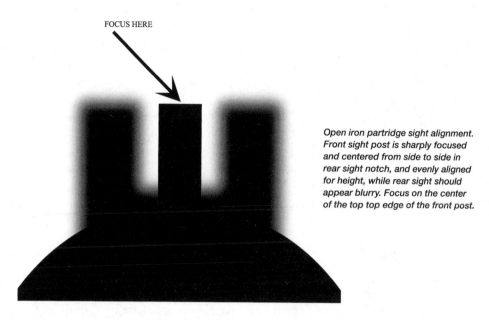

Open iron partridge sight alignment. Front sight post is sharply focused and centered from side to side in rear sight notch, and evenly aligned for height, while rear sight should appear blurry. Focus on the center of the top top edge of the front post.

a hole, focusing on the front sight. The front sight (tip of the post or face of the bead) must be centered in the aperture and your eye must be centered behind the aperture, focusing on the front sight. Your eye has a natural capacity to cen-ter itself behind any hole through which you are looking, and this is the principle used. If you are focusing on the top of the front sight post or face of the front sight bead, as you should be (not the target, or the rear face of the front sight post), your

Iron rear aperture sight on M1 rifle.

Iron front protected post sight on M1 rifle.

ture) rear sight, you need to create this consistent anchor point for your face on the stock. This means having your face pressed against the stock at one particular place, depending upon the shooting position you're in. This is the "cheek weld." Small variations in face position will mean misalignment between the front and rear sights – a big no-no that will cause misses. If you look through the peep to the front sight, and let your eye settle into what feels like a natural position behind the rear sight that centers the front sight correctly in the rear sight aperture without thinking about it much, you should wind up in the right place. For consistency, you must be able to consistently re-create the same stock/face contact. You must not only find this face contact position, but replicate it exactly every time you assume that shooting position, and for every shot you fire from that position.

Often a problem is that we have brought the buttstock to our shoulder in

eye's automatic centering will result in the top of the front sight post or center of the front sight bead being placed in the center of the rear sight aperture. This is correct sight alignment with aperture sights. Don't try to look at the rear aperture itself.

A good many people have serious trouble with peep sights. They don't understand the centering issue, or try to look at the rear sight rather than through it, or have trouble getting a repeatable eye position behind the rear sight due to inconsistency with the mount and cheek weld. Remember that you look through the rear sight, essentially ignoring it, and at the front sight. Don't make a big deal of it – just look through the hole at the front sight in a relaxed and natural manner, and let your eye dictate where your face has to contact the stock to allow this to happen. This is how you train yourself to fine-tune your cheek weld to give you this eye/sights alignment instantly.

To consistently align your front and rear sights when using a peep (aper-

FOCUS HERE

Aperture iron sight alignment. Top of front post is in sharp focus and centered in blurry rear ring. Focus on the top center edge of the front post.

The "thumb weld," cheek to thumb, to raise my head higher.

the wrong place, forcing our head into the wrong position relative to the stock. Bringing the sights up in front of your eye, and the stock to your cheek, before planting the butt in your shoulder helps get the correct gun mount. In the prone position, I sometimes find that the stock comb is so low that resting my face on it has me staring at the rear receiver wall below the sight. So, I hook my thumb over the stock and rest my cheekbone on it. I call this the 'thumb weld.' Not as comfortable in recoil, but it raises my eye up to where it should be. This prevents craning my head upwards, which results in a varying position of my eye every shot, and sore neck muscles which lead to even less consistent eye placement. You may hear the words "stock weld" used as well in place of "cheek weld."

If you are having a tough time mastering the aperture sight, a good trick is to use some part of the front sight or rifle barrel to align with the rear sight aperture at its 6-o'clock edge. That is, get a proper alignment with the front sight as near centered in the aperture as you can, then see where the lower edge of the rear aperture "cuts off" the view of the front sight base or top of the barrel. Memorize this relationship and make sure it looks exactly the same for every shot. And before you fire, don't forget to transfer focus to the front sight.

Even with the right techniques, it can take a bit of work to get consistent, comfortable, and reflexive with a rear aperture sight. There is a small zone of uncertainty wherein your eye cannot be exactly, perfectly certain that the front sight is perfectly centered in the aperture. This zone of uncertainty represents alignment error, and the newer you are to peep sights (or the larger the peep sight hole), the larger this zone will be. With enough practice time and care with the physical indices of buttstock to shoulder and cheek weld, this zone of error will become so small as to be irrelevant in normal usage. Attaining this level of proficiency is extremely desirable. With it, you can use a GI rifle to reliably hit anything you can clearly see out to ranges so far you might not believe me. The Marines still teach rifle marksmanship with iron sights out to 500 meters (almost 550 yards), and both they and the Army used to teach it to past 1000 yards back around World War I!

The "ghost ring" rear aperture

Most commercial rear aperture sights designed for hunting or target shooting are made with a screw-in disk that sports a fairly small hole. This aids in centering your eye behind the center of the hole, but cuts down on the view through the hole. This can be detrimental in low light or while trying to follow a moving target. Larger disk holes are becoming more available these days from some manufacturers. These may take some getting used to for a shooter who is not at ease with aperture sights, but for one who is comfortable with them, they are about as precise as a small hole and much faster to use. A very large hole with a thin rim is called a "ghost ring", a term coined by Col. Jeff Cooper.

In use, the thin rim seems to vanish as the eye focuses on the front sight. The view through the rear sight ghost ring is almost unimpeded by the ring itself, and it is the fastest of all to use. This sort of sight was, and still is, commonly found on military rifles dating back to World War II and in some cases earlier, and on up through the present day examples. You can create your own ghost ring from most commercial sights (such as the Lyman 48 or Williams Guide) by simply unscrewing and removing the aperture disk and using its threaded mounting hole as a large aperture.

A good rear aperture sight, combined with a square-top front post, can be surprisingly precise on any target you can see clearly. Military and civilian target shooters have proven the capability of peep sights on the target range out to 1000 yards. The combination of speed and visibility through a ghost ring, along with a large front post, is particularly good for big and/or dangerous game (four-legged or two-legged) at close quarters where speed can mean the difference between your life or death.

This is the main thing when using any iron sights: watch the front sight! Keep your focus there, not on the target. I know I have said this more than once already, but it must become an ingrained reflex! There is a tendency among untrained shooters to watch the target. This will cause your shots to wander. Let the target blur slightly and keep your front sight sharp! If your shots are wandering high-low-right-left without any cause you can detect (no wind changes, your hold looked good, etc.), you may have lost your front sight focus. This also may be the case if your shots seem to form two distinct groups. One group is formed when properly focusing on your sight, the other from improperly focusing on the target. Also, this two-group ef-

Iron rear ghost ring aperture sight, a Lyman with its disk removed, on a Winchester 94.

fect is often the result of the butt moving slightly from its original position against your shoulder, changing your cheek weld and therefore sight alignment. This often happens when firing a string of several shots with a powerful rifle, especially at long range. The longer the distance, the more small errors become large in effect on the target.

Sight picture

There are three main ways you can hold the front sight against a bullseye target. The first is the 6-o'clock hold. The top of the post is just under the bottom center edge of the target. You may just touch the black, or leave a thin line of white between the top of the post and the target black. If your eyes are not very good, it can be hard to tell which is which. The thin line of white is a good dividing line but must be of consistent width for every shot.

Your rifle should be zeroed (covered later) to hit the center of the bullseye with this hold, so you will be hitting higher than your front sight tip. It is help-

Focus on the front sight!

ful to know just how high in minutes of angle/sight clicks (covered below) this hitting higher is, so you can easily adjust back and forth between hitting the bullseye center with a six o'clock hold, or hitting something else with a dead-on, center-of-mass hold. This distance of hitting higher is controlled, obviously, by the black bullseye radius, and can change from target type to target type and/or distance to distance. In the sport of high-power rifle bullseye for example, it is the same angular divergence at all three distances of 200, 300, and 600 yards: three minutes of angle.

The second way is the "flat tire" hold. The tip of the post intrudes upward about one-quarter of the way into the bull. Rifle zeroing as above: the round should hit bullseye center.

The last is the dead-on center-of-mass hold. The top surface of the post comes up to the center of the target. The bullet should strike right where the top edge of the front sight appears. This is how your rifle should be zeroed at that distance.

I prefer the 6-o'clock hold with a hairline of white on a bullseye target because it gives me a clear contrast between the black front sight and the white part of the target, and a clear contrast between the edge of the sight and the edge of the bull. Holding into the black can get tricky, because you now see black-against-black without a clear dividing reference and it becomes hard to make sure your sight is in exactly the same place from shot to shot.

On a game animal (or terrorist...), use the dead-on center-of-mass hold and put the top surface of the front sight post against the point you want to hit, unless you are holding over for extended ranges. With a bead, use the center of the bead to cover the spot you wish to hit. Given the size of the bead, this pretty well limits this sort of use to about 150 yards or so, unless your target is large and your eyes keen. You might be able to use the top of the bead like the top of the post, but be-

Six o'clock hold on a bullseye target with iron Partridge sights. Focus on the top center edge of the front sight.

Six o'clock hold on a bullseye target with aperture iron sights. Focus on the top center edge of the front sight. Note that the target is not centered in the rear aperture.

Center of mass hold on a bullseye target with iron Partridge sights. Focus on the top center edge of the front sight.

Center of mass hold on a bullseye target with aperture iron sights. Focus on the top center edge of the front sight.

ing curved it makes for a difficult reference point from one shot to another. If so, make sure you have your rifle zeroed that way, otherwise you will be shooting very low if it is zeroed for bead center.

A little-known facet of the iron front sight post on a military rifle is that its di-

mensions are often designed to help the soldier range his target. The old M1 Garand front sight width subtends (covers) eight inches at 100 yards distance. At 250 yards this corresponds to 20 inches of covered width. This is roughly the width of a man (enemy soldier) seen facing you

Center of mass hold with factory open iron sights. Focus on the front bead face.

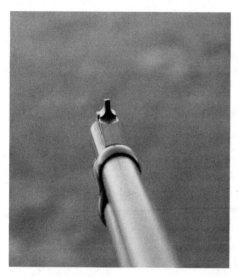

Using iron sights? This is your best friend.

from the front. With the rifle zeroed at this distance, an enemy that is the same size or wider than the front sight means you can hold dead-on and hit. If the enemy is smaller in width than your front sight, then it is beyond your zero distance and might require some aim adjustment to hit. The old British Enfield No. 4 front sight post was designed to look as tall as a man seen from a 400-yard distance. If you have such a rifle it is worth doing some experimentation comparing your front sight to various objects at various distances, as it makes for a handy reference that works at a glance.

The main requirements of iron sight use are to have that reproducible, consistent face/eye placement every shot, and to focus on the tip of the front sight. You will probably find that due to differences of head and body position relative to the rifle, you may have slight changes in shot placement from one position to another, especially between prone and all the other positions. This is the reason that

a sighting zero shot from a benchrest is really only a starting point.

When aiming, make sure both your eye and your mind are focused sharply on your front sight. Be aware of exactly where it is relative to the target and use the principles described in the following chapters on position shooting to keep it in the right place.

SCOPES

There are a few issues that need to be addressed here: Scope position, parallax, field of view vs. power, the concept of minutes of angle, and reticles.

Positioning

Scopes require the same care in eye position and face placement as an aperture sight. Most people set their scopes too far back, because they only shoot from standing or from the bench. In either case the head is erect and not too far forward of being directly over the pelvis. This allows a more rearward scope position. However, when a position like sitting or prone is taken, the body position puts the head further forward of the rest of the torso, and closer to the scope. This allows recoil to give you a very painful whack in the eyebrow with the rear of the scope. This will not help you avoid flinching!

Once you get past the notion of shooting only from the bench or from standing, you will realize that your body angle will bring your face into whacking range of your scope in recoil, so you will want to move the scope forwards a bit in the rings. You will want the rear of the scope to be about even with the rear of the trigger guard. This can be difficult to achieve with current scope and mount setups,

Rear end of scope even with rear of trigger guard. This prevents "scope eye" in prone and sitting.

due to the wide variable power ring on most variable scopes. You may need to get what are called extension rings, which offset the ring forwards from the base attachment point. You can get these for both the front and rear rings. You may also replace your current mount and ring setup with a Picatinny rail, which allows for different ring positioning along the length of the rail.

Eyepiece focus

The rear lens of the scope can be rotated on its threads to change its position forwards or rearwards. This should be set to focus the crosshairs sharply. It then becomes easy to judge your crosshairs position against the target. As with irons, be acutely aware of the precision of your aim and where your crosshairs are relative to your aiming point.

Parallax

Parallax is an optical phenomenon which may induce aiming error if the shooter is not careful. Every scope is focused at a certain distance. When viewing a target at this focus distance, small deviations of your eye from the center of the field of view will not matter. But at other distances, these small movements of your eye off-center will actually result in the crosshairs moving relative to the target. This is aiming error, or parallax. So, it pays to know the distance your scope has been focused to be parallax free. Usually, a big-game scope is focused at about 150 yards and a rimfire scope at about 50 yards, but this can vary by manufacturer or even by scope.

You can test this by placing your rifle on a benchrest such that it can be aligned with a target without you having to hold it there. Curl up behind it in firing position and without disturbing the rifle's position, look through the scope and move your eye from side to side and up and down slightly. If your target is placed at the parallax-free distance, you will see the crosshairs stay steady on the target. If at some other distance, you will see the crosshairs appear to move relative to the target in a direction opposite that of your eye's direction of motion.

You can buy basic hunting scopes (as opposed to specialized target, varmint, or sniper scopes) with an adjustable focus ring on the front bell. These are called adjustable objective scopes, which allow you to dial out parallax from short range to infinity – if you have the time to do so before the shot.

In reality, parallax is best dealt with by developing such a consistent cheek weld that your eye is always centered behind the scope no matter what position you are in. This, of course, takes quite a bit of position practice time – but does not necessarily require a lot of shooting, especially once you begin to get the cheek weld down, since you can do it with dry fire.

Power and field of view

Power and field of view are related in inverse proportion. Most people love high-powered magnification, but often give little thought to the fact that this greatly reduces field of view. One of my friends long had a 24x scope on his varmint rifle, and used to try to shoot jackrabbits running through thick cactus at short range. He would spend a long time looking for the speeding jack in the tiny field of view, and not get many shots off.

The primary consideration here is what kind of terrain you plan to hunt. In thick cover you will be making closer shots, often on a moving and partially obscured animal. You need all the field of view you can get to keep track of a moving animal under these conditions, yet high magnification is not necessary to see the target. At long ranges in open country the opposite is generally true. This should be glaringly obvious to everyone, but there will always be the fellow who turns his 3x9 scope up to 9 and leaves it there forever, even when entering dark timber. If you have a variable scope, keep track of where the magnification is set. You may want to leave it at the lower numbers in case you jump an animal at short range. At long ranges you will usually have the time to dial up the power if you have to before engaging the target. Just remember to turn it down again when you are through with that particular situation. In heavy cover up close, a small field of view due to excess magnification will make it very difficult to quickly pick up a partially-obscured, moving animal at close range, and may cost you the opportunity.

One thing to think about (for a big game rifle anyway) is to make your choice of a variable scope dependent upon the lower number, not the higher. Guys just love bigger numbers in anything, but it can work against you. You really don't need very high magnification for big game at normal ranges; eight or even six power will work fine on an antelope-sized target at 300 yards. Yet, sometimes having a power setting of 2x or 2.5x makes all the difference in thick, dark timber at the edges of legal shooting light. Some guys will put a 4-14x on a deer rifle, and that's

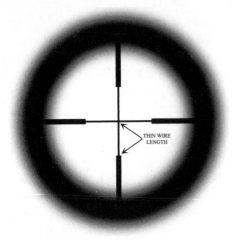

Common Duplex type reticle. We are interested in the thin wire length from intersection down to thick transition.

Center of mass hold with Duplex type reticle.

fine if 4x isn't too high a power for the conditions hunted. Give serious consideration to the cover and light conditions that you will be hunting.

My .270 wears a 2.5-8x scope, my .35 Whelen a 1.75-6x, and my .243 has a 3-9x. When I hunt with any of them they are turned down to at or near minimum in anticipation of a close-range surprise, and at this setting I can still hit anything I need to well past 200 yards. And while I should have plenty of time to crank up the power on a very distant target, it is almost a guarantee that if a buck breaks cover at 30 yards, I both won't be able to find him in the tiny field of view of a scope set at or near max power, nor have the time to crank the power down when it's set too high.

There is a reason the 3-9x is such a popular choice, after all, and if you have one, you might want to keep it set on 3x and frequently check it, especially after having turned it up for some specific look. Also, it is not generally a wise idea to use

your scope for scanning or target identification, since you are pointing a loaded rifle along with it. A compact 8x binocular hanging around your neck is much better suited and will prevent you from forgetting to lower your scope power down from 9x after using it to examine something.

Another popular feature is the 50mm front objective lens. This gathers quite a bit of extra light and can help the shooter see better at the edges of legal shooting light. However, it requires the scope to be mounted in high rings, and often requires the shooter to raise his head so far as to pull his cheek away from the stock. This can lead to head and eye placement problems in the gun mount, so be wary of such things. Leupold is now manufacturing a 50mm objective scope, which has a semicircular divot cut out of it at the bottom to clear the barrel at normal mounting height. Generally a 40mm to 44mm front lens diameter, combined with the lowest power setting, will let you see what you need to see during legal light conditions.

Scope reticles

Depending upon type, you may be able to use the reticle in your scope for either judging range or holding off. While manufacturers are increasingly offering a choice of different styles, the single most common type remains the Duplex type. So, let's look at what this offers us in the way of range-finding and hold-over assistance.

What you need to find out is the distance (at the target) between the intersection of the crosshairs and the transition point from thin crosshair wire to thick crosshair wire. The easiest way to do this is to use a target with a one-inch grid printed on it at 100 yards. Set the rifle on a benchrest and notice how many inches on the grid are covered by the length of the thinner wire, from intersection to thick wire transition. If your scope is a variable, then this number will probably change with each magnification power. To simplify matters, you can do this exercise at the highest power setting (which you will probably be using for your longest shots) and at the setting you normally use for general hunting.

Write down the number for each power you check. Remember that each inch at 100 yards is effectively the same as a minute of angle. We want to reference this number from here on as being in minutes of angle, not inches. This is important because the number of inches of this distance varies with our distance to the target, but the MOA value remains constant at all distances. This gives us only one number to memorize, instead of multiple different numbers of inches for different distances. Let's call this number the thin-wire MOA.

Now that you know this, what can you do with it? Let's say a deer's body is about 18 inches from top of shoulder to bottom of chest. Say you put the scope on a deer and its body fills the space from the crosshairs intersection held at the top of its shoulder to the top of the lower thick wire held at the base of its chest. You check your thin-wire MOA dimension for that scope power setting and find that it is six MOA. At what distance does 18 inches equal six MOA? The unit of the answer will be in hundreds of yards. So, six into 18 goes three times, or 300 yards. Cross checking our answer, we realize that at 300 yards one minute of angle equals about three inches. Three inches divided into 18 inches equals six, our known thin-wire MOA coverage number for that scope power setting.

As you can see, you need to have a pretty good guess at the size of the object you are measuring this way. If you know the body height of the game animal you are after, you can spend some time at the range with your scope, and determine at what power setting and at what range (using minutes of angle) the thin-wire MOA distance will bracket that animal's body height. Once you get the thin-wire MOA coverage for each scope power, you can calculate the power setting and range that your quarry animal's body will be perfectly bracketed by the reticle. When you see that game animal off in the distance, you can set your scope for that power setting, bracket the animal, and tell whether it is nearer than, right at, or further than your calculated bracket distance, thus giving you a rough range measurement.

Another way to use this thin-wire MOA is as a holdover aid. One day, I was testing my .22 rimfire rifle at 100 yards with the 3x9 scope set on about eight power. With a 75-yard dead-on zero, my shot group fell some five or so inches below the crosshair intersection on the target. It so happened, by sheer chance, that the group was centered on the thick-to-thin transition point on the lower crosshair wire. I realized that at this power setting at the 100 yard distance, I could simply use this thick-to-thin transition point as a handy 100-yard sight. If I were to lower the scope power setting, then this thin-wire MOA would be larger, and be useful as a holdover for even further distances.

So, if you know your bullet's drop at ranges further out than your zeroing distance (and know the distance to the target to give you the drop number), you can convert this drop in inches to minutes of angle, and perhaps – depending on your scope's design and power range – simply dial in the power that gives you that same value for thin-wire MOA, and use the thick-thin transition point of the lower wire like a post iron sight. If this is not possible, then perhaps you can find a power that gives a thin-wire MOA of double your bullet drop MOA, and hold with the target exactly between the crosshairs intersection and the thick-thin transition point.

These sorts of calculations take a few seconds, but on very long shots, your intended target is usually unaware of your presence, so you may find the time to pull them off. It is worth the time to learn, since it beats guesswork by a country mile, unless you prefer using the scope adjustments instead. If you are going to do the latter, test your scope on the range with back-and-forth adjustments to see if it does indeed track accurately to the changes you dial in, and back again to your starting point. Not all scopes do. This is called "shooting a box": using a large paper target, fire two shots, then crank one knob (either elevation or windage) a few minutes of angle in one direction, then fire two more. Repeat in a direction at a right angle, and continue until you should adjust back to your original setting, then fire two more. You should have four groups making a square, with the holes at the corners, and the last two shots should be right on the first two.

WHAT YOU CAN LEARN FROM YOUR SIGHTS

Your eye and mind focus on your front sight/crosshairs is critical to successful shooting. Here is a list of some things your sight will tell you:

1) Whether you are focusing sharply on a front iron sight (sharp not blurry sight).

2) Whether you are properly aligned on your target (proper sight picture).

3) Whether you have proper sight alignment (iron sights and eye centered behind scope).

4) How large or small your wobble zone is (how well you are executing the position).

5) Where your Natural Point of Aim is (covered later).

6) Depending on your sight configuration, ranging distance to target.

7) Where your shot went (calling the shot).

8) Whether or not you are blinking as you press the trigger (you should see your sight lift in recoil if you are not flinching).

Making it all work together.

9) If your support elbow is under the rifle correctly (vertical, not diagonal motion of the rifle sight while breathing).

All these things are critical to diagnose what you are doing wrong and confirm what you are doing right. Learn to read the information your sights show you and put it to use! Paying attention the above list on every shot will reap you huge advances in your shooting.

CALLING THE SHOT

If you keep your eye on the front sight and achieve a proper trigger release, you should know where the sight was when you fired. Where the sight goes, the shot goes, and you can "call" its probable point of impact based on your seeing where your front sight was in relation to the target at the instant of firing. You absolutely need to learn how to do this because it is about the only thing that allows self-analysis and self-correction. First, if you saw the sight at the instant of discharge, then you are likely performing correct trigger management and are not making the usual mistakes. Second, if you know that you threw a shot in a given direction, you can tell the difference between a shot that went wide due to your aim error, and one that went wide for some other reason. If you don't know when you pulled one, you can't even determine which problem you need to solve.

ADJUSTING YOUR SIGHTS

When adjusting iron sights, move the rear sight in the direction you want your group to move, or the front sight in the opposite direction. When adjusting a scope, obey the arrow directions on the turrets under the caps.

THE "GOLDEN RULE" OF SIGHT USE

I've saved the best for last. The primary purpose of your sights is to tell you when to press the trigger. If you are using your sights correctly, you should recognize a correct sight picture when you see it: front and rear sights (if using irons) properly aligned with each other and with the target, or the scope crosshairs intersection right where it needs to be. Obviously you should not apply trigger pressure unless and until you are happy with what your eye is seeing in the sight picture. This includes both alignment and steadiness. Proper trigger management and steadiness are covered in later chapters. What you need to discipline yourself with right now is the notion that the sight picture is the boss of the trigger finger. That is, your finger is slave to your brain which is slave to what the eye sees. If the sight picture is not right, or the rifle is jerking and twitching all over the place, DON'T PRESS THE TRIGGER!!

This simple concept will prevent an awful lot of misses. It forces you to correct the actual problem, whether it is aiming error or position error, rather than just trying to jerk the trigger at what you think is the right time and place in the wild wobbling and hoping for the best. If you only press the trigger on a perfect sight picture that is holding fairly steady within your desired impact zone, guess what – you'll probably never miss. You should now know how to get a perfect sight picture; how to get that steady is covered in the following chapters. Remember: if your sight picture isn't as perfect as you can get it, make it so before you fire the shot.

CHAPTER 5

TRAJECTORY AND EXTERIOR BALLISTICS

This chapter is not intended to be a study of exterior ballistics, which is a major undertaking in and of itself, but rather a general guide to understanding the basic principles involved, and to give the rifle shooter a starting point for further exploration. It is my intent here to get you started on that road with the right ideas and a general understanding of what to expect from your own rifle/ammo combination, so that you can understand the behavior of a bullet in flight and the forces acting upon it, and so understand the shape of its trajectory and come up with a reasonable choice of zero distance. For more inquisitive (and mathematically inclined) minds, I suggest acquiring a copy of the Sierra Bullets reloading manual, which often (depending upon the edition) has a splendidly detailed section on the physics of exterior ballistics (including drop/zero charts for every one of their bullets).

Where we choose to zero our rifle will control what kind of trajectory we have. This depends on the velocity of the cartridge, the size of our target, and how far out we want to push the beginning of rapid bullet drop.

There are a number of considerations. Since the barrel of a conventionally-sighted rifle will be pointed slightly upwards relative to the line of the sights, the bullet starts out from the muzzle at this upward angle. Gravity acts on the bullet the instant it leaves the muzzle, making it fall away from the line from which the barrel directed it. With a properly zeroed firearm, the bullet will still rise enough to cross up through the line of sight (even as it falls away from the bore line), climb up over the sight line as it reaches the top of its arc (called the maximum ordinate), then fall back down through the line of sight. It is the second, further intersection of the bullet path with the line of sight that is the "zero" point. Once beyond the zero point, the bullet will generally drop at an accelerated rate.

There are two important points to consider here. The further out you want the zero point to be, the higher the arc of the

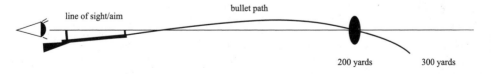

Bullet trajectory

maximum ordinate over your sight line will be. This raises the question of how high this should be. Too high and you risk shooting over your target at distances closer than your zero point, or having to do a mental calculation of your range and trajectory in order to hold under your desired impact point.

The second point to consider is that gravity is a constant force, which makes objects fall faster and faster and faster – accelerating downwards over time. This means that the longer the bullet is in the air ("ballistic"), the faster its downward motion becomes. This is one reason why drop at long distance is so severe. The other is that the bullet's forward motion slows (due to air resistance) over time. Thus, as time goes by (which means greater downrange motion of the bullet), the bullet's forward motion per second slows down while its downward motion per second speeds up. The combination of these two phenomena produces the sharp downward hook in trajectory beyond zero point that makes range estima-

tion at long distance so crucial.

The best answer to this is to pick a zero point distance that will keep your maximum ordinate height just small enough to be able to aim at your given target size dead center and still hit it with a shot taken at maximum ordinate distance, where your bullet will be at the top of its arc above the line of sight. This concept is called "point blank." It allows you to not have to think about aim adjustments for distance, for the longest possible distance. When you pick a given point blank zero range, it is dictated by the mid-range rise of the bullet above sight line being within your desired target zone with a dead-center hold, and when your bullet drops down below your line of sight (at a further distance than your zero distance) to the extent of just barely being within your target zone using a dead-center hold, you now have your maximum point blank range. This, of course, is dependent upon the total height of your intended zone of impact combined with the bullet's velocity.

size of target

This hit at maximum bullet rise with dead-center hold
This hit at zero distance with dead-center hold
This hit at maximum point blank range with dead center hold

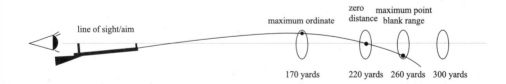

line of sight/aim

zero distance
maximum point blank range

maximum ordinate

170 yards   220 yards   260 yards   300 yards

POINT BLANK ZEROING: By using the height of the target as a gauge, we can get the furthest zero distance possible which allows a dead-center hold without the bullet going over the target at its maximum rise (maximum ordinate) distance.

How point blank zeroing works.

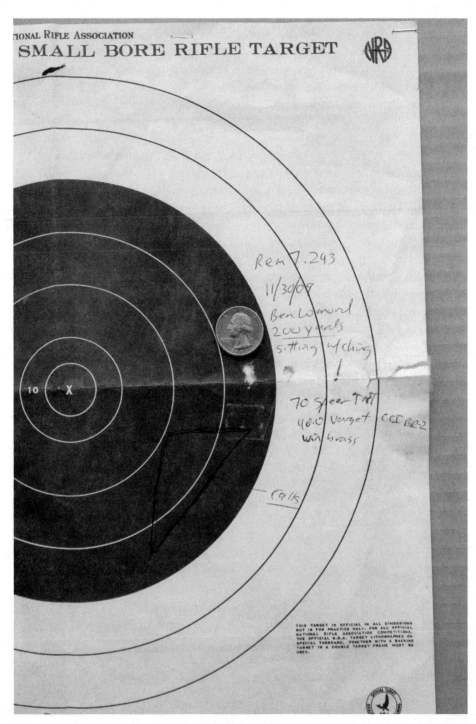

Zero checking my .243. Three careful rounds from open-leg sitting with tight Ching sling. The corners of the triangle were my shot calls. My zero was off, but I'll take that group size (at 200 yards!!) any day! Just don't ask me to repeat it. That day I was the windshield, not the bug.

Say your quarry - a deer - sports a kill zone of about an 8-inch diameter. You want to zero your rifle at a distance that allows you to aim dead center on this 8-inch circle and not miss high at maximum ordinate (maximum bullet rise above line of aim) range. Since modern cartridge velocities allow us to choose a zero point somewhere between 150 and 250 yards, and maximum ordinate point will be closer than this, and since we have to take average rifle/ammo group size at maximum ordinate range into account, let's allow for an inch of extra bullet height if our rifle shoots a higher than perfect shot. This means we want a zero distance that will put our maximum ordinate height at no more than three inches above our sight line for a "perfect" shot, which allows a shot an inch higher than this (remember, we have to factor in the high shots in overall group size) to still nick our 8-inch circle at its upper edge when fired with a dead-center hold at maximum ordinate distance.

Okay, you say, so what distance will that be for my .30-30/.270/.300 Earthshaker? There are two ways to do this. For exact bullet paths, there are several ballistics calculators available on the internet that will take into account such variables as sight height over bore center, altitude, air temperature, and humidity (which is nice for 1000-yard shooting, but not entirely necessary for shots under 300). Some of them will even calculate a point blank zero distance for you if you supply a maximum bullet rise number. You enter the relevant data (knowing your actual, measured muzzle velocity is crucial to an accurate answer) and the program spits out the answer. A similar

result can be had if you can grab a reloading manual off your bookshelf and read the external ballistics tables in the back for your bullet. The Sierra Bullets rifle reloading manual lists point-blank zero distances for their bullets at all practical velocities. Even if you are not using their product, matching type, form, and weight will give you a good workable approximation.

Failing all this, a good rule of thumb for an 8-inch target diameter is to zero about 2.5 inches high at 100 yards, which (depending on your bullet's velocity) should put you about two inches high at 200 with cartridges over 2600 feet per second velocity, and dead-on somewhere between 220 and 250 yards (your actual zero distance). With a center hold, your bullet will be roughly three inches below your crosshairs at somewhere between 250-285 yards, again depending on your velocity. The latter number is your maximum point-blank distance (not actual zero distance). At any range from muzzle to your maximum point-blank range, simply hold dead-center on the animal's 8-inch kill zone (heart/lung area) and shoot. Your bullet will impact somewhere within this zone, either high in the zone at the maximum ordinate range, center at zero distance, or low in the zone at max point-blank range or at very close range (under 25 yards).

This concept is quite advantageous. By extending your hold-center range to its maximum distance, it reduces the mental work you may face in the field by greatly reducing the number of incidences of having to do a trajectory and aim adjustment in your head. All you have to do is determine whether the critter is in-

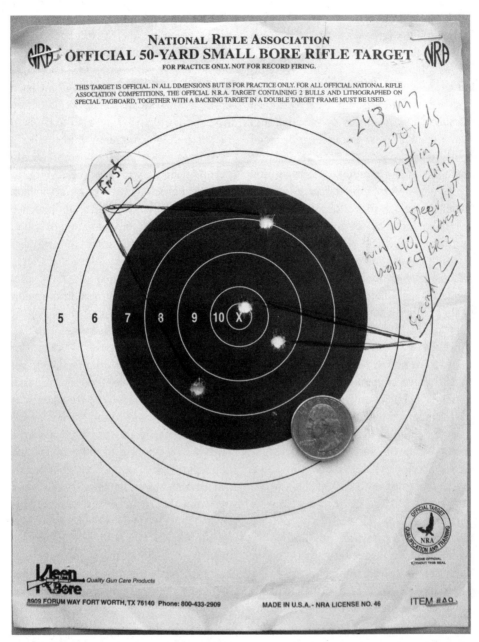

A more usual 200 yard zero check for my .243. This rifle seems to shoot by itself. What is possible with a really good sitting position and tight loop sling.

side your max point blank range before firing. If it is, hold center and shoot. If not, then you have to start calculating range and holdover (or, just stalk closer to within point-blank distance).

An alternative is, in more general (and less efficient) terms, to take the various velocities, group them by ranges of about 400 or so feet per second, and come up with a workable zero distance that will get you very close. This latter method, while not precise, is based on a century of observations of cartridge performance, so it will work as a guideline.

For example: bullets in the 1800-2300 fps range (like the .45/70, .30-30, .35 Remington) are best zeroed at about 150-175 yards, with about a two- to two-and-a-quarter-inch height above aimpoint at 100 yards and about five to six inches of drop at 200. Rounds in the 2300-2700 fps range can be zeroed at 200 yards, with about a one and three quarter to two inch height above aimpoint at 100 yards and about eight to eleven inches of drop at 300. Rounds in the 2700-3100 fps range can be zeroed at 225 yards (about 200 meters) with the same 100 yard height as the previous example, and about five to six inches of drop at 300. This is often good enough to get you started with shooting at 100 yards to verify correct impact position relative to aim point, which should translate into a good hit on a deer-sized kill zone target at 50 to 75 yards beyond your zero distance. It is, however, a rough-approximation method, and will not have quite as far a point-blank range.

Obviously the best thing to do is to find a range that lets you shoot your zero at the exact distance you want it to be, as well as allowing both a 100-yard distance check and also a distance of 50 yards or 100 yards past your zero point for complete, holes-in-paper verification. It is well worth the gasoline money (and club membership cost) to travel to such a range if you can find one, especially if you have either a low-velocity, rainbow-trajectory rifle or any rifle that you want to shoot at ranges a bit longer than normal.

If you want to really become an expert field shot, one of the smartest things you can do is to get the best point-blank zero for your rifle that correctly matches the size of the target you intend to shoot, calculate your maximum point blank distance (you can use free internet-available software to accomplish all this), and then learn to judge your maximum point blank range by eye.

JUDGING RANGE

This is a difficult art to master, yet quite critical. My method is to learn very well what 100 yards (or meters, if you prefer) looks like, and then to "block out" distance by this amount. It works fairly well to about 250-300 yards, which happens to be about where your maximum point blank distance should wind up. After that, it becomes very sketchy, which happens to be about where bullet drop starts to accelerate and knowing the distance to the target precisely becomes very important. There are other methods, such as extending your hand at arm's length and using the width of a finger to compare to objects of known size. Whichever you pick, it takes a lot of practice to nail down. And as mentioned previously, your front sight or scope reticle can be put to good use.

If you own a laser rangefinder, use it to teach your eye to become a good judge of range. This will pay enormous dividends on distant targets when you find its battery is dead halfway up the mountain.

BALLISTIC COEFFICIENT

While we are on the topic of bullet flight, it seems appropriate to mention ballistic coefficient (B.C.). This is a number that represents the aerodynamic efficiency of a bullet compared to a theoretical "standard" bullet shape. The higher the number, the more sleek and aerodynamic the bullet is. This allows it to overcome air resistance more easily with reduced velocity loss. This translates into shorter flight time to a given distance, which in turn yields less wind drift and less drop (flatter trajectory) compared to a similar weight bullet at similar velocity but with a lower B.C.

Obviously the flat-point type of bullet used by a .30-30 or .45-70 lever gun will have a very poor B.C. Next best are the round nose bullets. Both these types will shed velocity very rapidly with concomitant negative effect on trajectory out past 175 to 200 yards.

Bullets of the spire-point (straight conical taper pointed nose) and spitzer (slightly curved taper pointed nose) shapes will have a higher B.C. A pointed bullet with a tapered base (boat tail) is usually the sleekest shape, with the highest B.C.

Flat-pointed or very blunt round-nose bullets will have a definite bad effect on downrange velocity retention, and will require some careful attention to the bullet's trajectory even at medium ranges – say, 150 to 200 yards. However, for

most pointed type bullets used at normal big-game hunting range, ballistic coefficient variations make very little noticeable difference inside 300 yards. When ranges get out to 400 yards, the high B.C. bullets begin to show a slight advantage, usually about an inch less drop and about the same less wind drift. Example: Sierra lists the difference between their .270 130 grain flat base and 130 grain boat tail hunting bullets at 3000 feet per second, 200 yard zero, as the boat tail shooting .75-inch flatter at 400 yards, with about 1.5-inches less wind drift (10 mph crosswind), and lists the difference between the .30 150 grain flat base and boat tail at 2900 fps as being virtually the same as the .270 bullets.

As you can see, a plain old flat base bullet will work just fine to whack Bambi all the way out to 300 yards, and even beyond. You will not be able to tell the difference between a flat base and a boat tail even at the distance listed in the example above. Think about it: at 400 yards, the difference between the two types of bullet is still considerably smaller than the area of target covered by the intersection of your crosshairs! So, if you just have to have a boat tail anyway, go right ahead. But now you know what they really do at "normal" hunting ranges.

As the range increases beyond here, the difference between a high B.C. bullet such as a match grade boat tail and a garden-variety spitzer/spire point flat base becomes very noticeable, especially in the wind drift resistance category. For long-range varmint shooting, target shooting at any distance from 300 yards out, and "tactical" (sniper) shooting, the high B.C. bullet greatly reduces wind drift and flattens the trajectory a bit as well, making good hits quite a bit easier than a garden-variety flat base hunting bullet. At 1000 yards, here's what happens in the above examples: .270/130 hunting bullet specs as above, the boat tail has just over 27 inches less drop and about 13 ½ inches less wind drift than the flat base. The .30/150 numbers run 22 inches less drop for the boat tail and about 8 ½ inches less wind drift.

A match (target competition) grade boat tail bullet will be a further improvement still – especially a heavier bullet. A .30 190 grain Sierra Matchking boat tail at 2600 feet per second starting speed and a 200 yard zero will have 358 ½ inches of drop and 87 inches of 10 mph cross-wind drift at 1000 yards versus 353 inches of drop and 112 ½ inches wind drift for the 150 grain "hunting" boat tail. This illustrates certain advantages of a bullet that is heavy for its caliber at long range. Heavy for caliber means longer length. A longer bullet can be given a sleeker nose shape and boat tail, raising its B.C. number. Its extra weight, though making it start out a bit slower, helps it to hold onto its velocity better through greater

momentum, which helps make even better use of its higher B.C., and also better resists the sideways push of wind. As the above example shows, a 300 fps advantage in starting speed by the 150 grain bullet only translates into a five and a half inch trajectory advantage all the way out at 1000 yards, and the wind drift difference is enough to completely miss the 10-ring on a 1000 yard target – or an enemy soldier.

Range to a stationary target can be known, as on a target range, measured with an optical or laser rangefinder, or even swagged, but whatever it is, it is fixed; you make your estimation and adjust accordingly. Wind is a devilish variable, which means your amount of estimation error can be huge, so having a bullet with reduced drift helps.

But, since this book is not about long-range shooting, shouldn't we instead ask if heavy or light bullets are appropriate in a given situation? And what kind of bullet should we be using for our hunting purposes? We'll look at bullets and their terminal (impact) effects in a later chapter.

CHAPTER 6

MANAGING THE TRIGGER

Managing the trigger correctly is what makes or breaks the shooter. It is probably the most important act in firing a good hit. Bear in mind that is a very simple physical technique, but often we burden this act with all manner of mental and emotional baggage that is far more damaging to accuracy than it has to be. Fear of recoil is usually the worst problem, though nerves caused by "buck fever," the stress of competition, trying to force a difficult shot through bad technique, or dislike of having someone watch you perform are nearly as bad. In all these cases, the mind is doing way more work than it needs to do to perform the simple act of firing a shot, and all of this extra work has negative effects.

When placing your hand on the rifle and finger on the trigger, try to get the center of the end joint pad of your trigger finger on the trigger first, then let the hand fall where it may on the stock. This will help you get a straight-to-the-rear trigger pull, which minimizes any extraneous motion imparted to the rifle.

The usual bad physical habits are yanking or jerking the trigger. The physical motion must be smooth and gentle, with only the trigger finger moving and the rest of the hand staying relaxed. The finger should pull straight rearwards without any side-to-side or up-or-down motion. Using the center of the pad of the end joint usually gives the best combination of leverage and sensitivity.

Of the mental habits, the worst is flinching. This is a jerking of the body in anticipation of recoil as the trigger is being pulled, which jerks the gun way off target before the shot is fired: a push of your body against the gun in an attempt to counter recoil. It deflects the impact of the shot because this push is delivered before the bullet leaves the muzzle, usually before the round actually fires. The reason for this is when the mind delivers the command to the trigger finger to start pressing the trigger, the mind is fully aware that the result of this will produce a recoil impulse. If you quickly and firmly press the trigger (or worse, mash or jerk it) there is almost no time delay between the pressing of the trigger and the recoil. Your subconscious mind will therefore cause your hands (if shooting a handgun) or arms and upper body (when shooting a rifle) to push against the firearm at the same time as your finger is pressing the trigger. The result is a motion that deflects the gun muzzle before the shot is fired. The flinch is not in reaction to a shot already fired, rather it is an

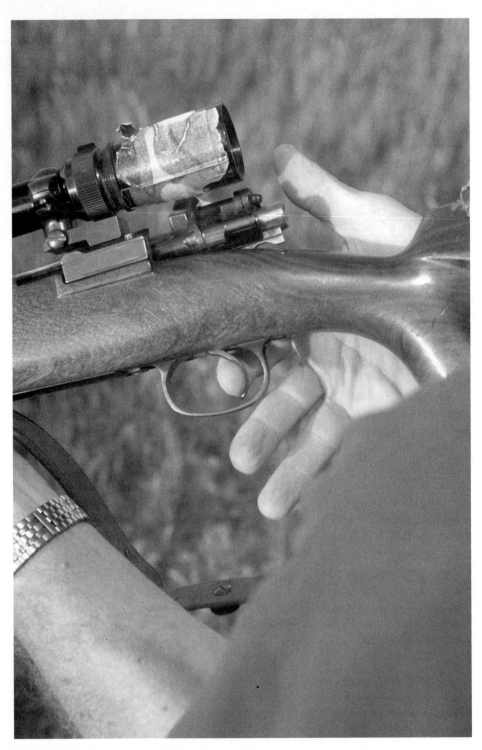

Where the trigger should touch your finger.

The hand rests on the stock based on correct finger placement on the trigger.

anticipation of the shot you are about to fire.

The classic drill for detecting a flinch is the "ball and dummy" drill. This involves having a partner load your firearm with a mix of live and dummy cartridges in a magazine firearm, or leaving some empty chambers in a revolver load, without the shooter seeing the details. The shooter simply fires shot after shot with the partner observing the shooter, and when a dummy round or empty chamber comes under the hammer, the partner will see clearly whether or not the shooter is flinching. Downward or forward twitch of the gun, jerking of the trigger hand, bucking of the trigger side shoulder, or an eye blink are the usual giveaways. This is worthwhile even if you think you have none of these issues, as nearly everyone who has them doesn't realize it!

The simplest cure for all this is the "surprise break": to gradually press the trigger straight rearwards in such a way that the discharge is a surprise, tensing only the trigger finger and not the rest of the hand. First take your time, then gradually speed up the process without losing the surprise factor. Empty and relax your mind during the shot. Dry fire works wonders for this. Remember, EVERY shot must be a surprise. In this fashion, your subconscious mind (which directs the flinch reflex) will not be able to discern just when the gun will fire, and therefore cannot create a flinch.

A good indicator that you are not flinching is if you can see your sights lift in recoil. A flinch usually contains an eye blink at the same time, so you will not see just what happened in that instant. However, if you see your sights jump and perhaps catch a bit of the flame of the muzzle blast, it means you are doing things right. And, seeing where your sights were at the moment of discharge means you can call where the shot went.

When pulling the trigger, make sure that the flexing of the trigger finger does not create contact with the rifle stock. This can push the stock sideways very slightly, with concurrent effect on your aim. Also, make sure you are pulling the trigger straight rearwards, and not pushing or pulling the gun sideways in the process. Make sure the trigger hand does not tense with the motion of the trigger finger; the finger should act with complete independence from the hand.

When starting the trigger press, concentrate on your sight picture and try to not think at all about the trigger press. Narrow your whole universe down to a little circle around your sight picture. If you can imagine that your job is to aim and that someone else will be pulling the trigger, you will be in a good frame of mind. The worst causes of trigger management troubles are almost always the mental ones.

BREATH CONTROL: RESPIRATORY PAUSE

When practicing your position, you will see that your sights move as you breathe. In prone and sitting, your sights should move straight down when you inhale, and come back up when you exhale. So, you'll need to pause your breathing to take the shot.

It is steadier and more naturally consistent to exhale all of your air first rather than to hold a full or partial breath. There is a slight pause after a normal exhalation called natural respiratory pause, where you will be quite motionless and relaxed for a few seconds. The nice thing about using this technique is that it is naturally and consistently repeatable without thinking about it, which works in your favor. Be aware that you will have only about eight seconds or so before oxygen deprivation ruins your performance. If you run out of air, stop, take another breath, and try again. Don't force the shot just so you can breathe again. Try to breathe from the lower abdomen instead of the upper chest. You will gain more air and disturb your body position less in all positions except prone.

Respiratory pause is where you want to time the trigger press. This will be very important to the consistency of your sight picture, and must be coordinated with another important technique called natural point of aim, covered in the next chapter.

TRIGGER FOLLOW-THROUGH

When shooting a semi-automatic firearm, the action cycles so fast that you will still be maintaining pressure on the trigger as the action closes. The trigger mechanism will be disconnected at this point. It will only reset itself after you release the trigger enough to let it move forwards the short distance required for mechanical reset.

Hold pressure on the trigger for just a half second or so after the shot, then release. This will keep your finger from being 'bounced' back against the trigger by forward rifle movement during post-recoil recovery, which could inadvertently fire another shot after the initial reset.

Learn the reset distance of your trigger and train your trigger finger to move for-

ward only this minimum necessary distance. Do not move your finger forward off the trigger completely, and especially do not fling your finger far forwards off the trigger to the front of the trigger guard. This is a wasteful and inefficient movement that requires a long motion out and then another one back to the trigger for any follow-up shot. Only release the trigger enough to reset its mechanism but do not add any more pressure, just maintain very slight finger contact with the trigger face. For a manually-operated rifle, of course, this generally does not apply, since working the action with the trigger hand cocks the striker and resets the trigger. The one exception to this is a pump-action, but in this case the action is both shooter-directed and much slower than a semi-auto.

A word about factory triggers is relevant here. Many, if not most, are abominable. What you want is a pull that is about 2.5 to 3.5 pounds in weight and as crisp as you can get. Crisp means there is no feeling of trigger motion, grating, or "mush" as the trigger is being pulled before the shot goes off. Factory triggers can either be adjusted or replaced by a competent gunsmith. Since the difference between "light and crisp" and "heavy and creepy" is the difference between a gun that is easy to shoot well and one that is a struggle to shoot well, this adjustment should not be overlooked.

MANUAL ACTION FOLLOW-THROUGH

Upon firing, immediately cycle the action, keeping the buttstock firmly in place in your shoulder, your face firmly against the stock, and eyes on sights, if the mechanism allows (a standard length or mag-

Lever rifle: shot is away, hammer is down, finger comes off trigger.

Keeping the rifle shouldered, cheek weld intact, eye behind sight, trigger finger straight, and rifle controlled with the support hand, work the lever firmly. Inhale at the same time.

Close lever with trigger finger still straight. Exhale at the same time.

Lifting bolt handle with outer edge of hand. Keep the rifle shouldered, cheek on stock, eye behind scope. Start inhaling.

Bolt handle lifted with outer edge of hand.

Sweeping bolt to rear with palm of hand. Don't smack your hat brim.

Reverse palm to push bolt forward. Start exhaling.

Palm closes bolt with outer edge of hand. Rifle, cheek, and eye still in firing position for follow-up shot. Your breathing should be at respiratory pause, ready to shoot.

Grasping bolt handle with fingers.

Lifting bolt handle with grasping fingers. Start inhaling.

Pulling bolt open with fingers. Again, watch out for your hat.

Bolt open with fingers, front view.

Base of thumb pushes bolt forward. Start exhaling.

Closing the bolt with grasping thumb. Respiratory pause.

num bolt rifle may require you to roll your face off the stock to save your nose).

Operating the gun from the shoulder instead of lowering it saves two or three seconds on a follow-up shot, and maintains the relationship between rifle and body from shot to shot. Work the mechanism vigorously; you aren't going to hurt it. Make sure the empty case extracts and ejects and the live round chambers with the action fully closed.

And, while working the action, inhale and exhale a quick short breath, so when you have chambered the next round you are ready to fire in sync with your respiratory pause. Remember to breathe!

There are a couple of different techniques for working a bolt smoothly and quickly. You can shift the outer edge (pinky finger side) of your firing hand to the bolt handle so your palm faces up, and lift the bolt up with the palm edge and back with the fingers, then rotate your hand so the palm faces toward the muzzle and hook the bolt between thumb and fore-finger to close it. Or, you can reach your trigger hand to grab the bolt between thumb and fore-finger/middle fingers and keep that grip for the open/close sweep. Learn the motions so that it is not up-back-forward-down, but rather a single sweeping arc to open, and again to close.

With practice you can develop a bolt stroke of close to one second simultaneous with an inhale/exhale cycle, all while keeping the rifle butt in your shoulder, your face on the stock, and eye behind the sights. If you want folks to think your manual rifle is a semi-auto, you can get there with practice.

Even when intending to fire only one shot, take a second aim at the target after cycling the action and before lowering the rifle. This is follow-through, which allows a lightning-fast second shot. Each shot is aim-fire-cycle-aim. This is extremely important. If you drop the rifle from your shoulder as soon as you shoot while looking downrange for the effect of your shot, you'll waste an inordinate amount of time. If you then need a second shot, the animal will likely be gone by the time you can fire. If you've done everything correctly with the first shot you shouldn't need a second, but if you do, you'll need it in a hurry. So, see if you're finished shooting at that target by looking through your sights. Get in the habit of working the action sharply, without short-stroking it, keeping the butt in your shoulder and face on the stock, and taking a second sight picture after every shot you take. It's a good insurance policy. Remember: AIM-FIRE-CYCLE-AIM. (Remember to breathe while cycling the action!) Only then do you either fire the second shot if necessary, or lower the rifle. Make this an automatic reflex.

CHAPTER 7

PRINCIPLES OF POSITION SHOOTING

When we achieve proper aiming and trigger control, we still need one more ingredient to accurately place a shot: a steady hold that keeps the sight on the desired aiming point. This eliminates the familiar condition of the sight zig-zagging all over, on and off the aiming point, while we try to time the instant to yank the trigger and hope to get a hit. Correct use of the appropriate shooting position is what provides this. Ideally, we want to achieve a hold so steady that our zone of wobbling is small enough to be inside our desired zone of impact.

Shooting aids are popular today, chiefly bipods and shooting sticks. The main reason these are so popular is the general lack of understanding of, or ability to execute, good old-fashioned position shooting. The modern attitude seems to be that with some sort of rest, learning position shooting is no longer necessary.

Ironically, in order to take the fullest advantage of bipods and sticks, you still need to be thoroughly grounded in position shooting theory, because bipods and sticks are only of limited use if your body is still swaying around. If the shoulder in contact with the rifle butt is moving, so will the muzzle be, regardless of your type of rest. The rest simply acts like a fulcrum over which the rifle pivots like a seesaw. So, even with an artificial rest like sticks or a bipod holding up the rifle fore-end, we still need to know the best way to stabilize our bodies to keep the butt-end of the rifle from moving.

Further, even though you may have a bipod stuck on all your rifles, you may end up shooting without one someday. Gadgets break, or you may be using a borrowed rifle. It pays to be able to shoot without being too dependent on gadgets doing the work for you. The sum of the principles in this book will help you become a better shot no matter what style you shoot.

The importance of proper position cannot be overstated. Selection and assumption of a proper position will determine how steady you can hold. First, we need to know which position to use for a given shot; second, we need the ability to assume that position correctly.

The former is easy: if you can't keep the motion of your front sight or crosshairs within the zone you want to hit, invoke Col. Jeff Cooper's dictum, "If you can get closer, get closer. If you can get steadier, get steadier." There is no reason to shoot standing up when squatting, kneeling, sitting, or even prone are viable, no matter how close or large the tar-

Open-leg sitting with loop sling, a great field position.

Kneeling with loop sling and a little field-expedient help for its weakest feature.

get. As the Colonel says, "The purpose of shooting is hitting."

Always pick the steadiest position that is workable in a situation. If you persist in rifle training, sufficient practice will educate you as to exactly what you can achieve from each position and what your range limitations are, and you will pick the proper one. Learning and memorizing each position's wobble zone size in minutes of angle should be part of your training program.

And yes, go ahead and use any suitable rest available when in the field. Remember that the thrust of this work is to teach you how to "do it all." I am not trying to wean you off your bipod as much as to show you how to operate very well without one, and to use these same principles to enhance any rested shooting you do.

PRINCIPLES

Proper use of position, along with the concept of natural point of aim and the shooting loop sling, form a solid foundation that allows us to put our aiming and trigger management skills to the best possible use. Natural point of aim, or NPA (covered below), holds your rifle precisely on target without you having to do any muscle work to keep the rifle aimed. The loop sling (covered in the next chapter) actually holds up the rifle for you. The shooting position, done correctly, allows maximum muscle relaxation and maximum bone support for maximum steadiness. This combination creates a high degree of steadiness with a low degree of effort. The end result of correct performance of all this is effortless aiming. This may sound impossible,

but I'm not kidding. Effortless aiming is quite possible in both prone and sitting positions – if you do everything related below correctly.

The first thing to remember about position shooting is that you want to minimize the use of tense muscle to hold the position, and instead allow your skeleton to take the greatest load of work. Bones don't get tired and start trembling. This principle allows the maximum amount of body relaxation, which not only reduces quivering but also fatigue. It is important to remember to always relax your body (and your mind) as much as possible in each position.

Another principle is the use of gravity instead of muscle. For example, in the sitting position, it is advantageous to apply an aggressive forward lean to the upper body, so that the weight of the torso settles onto the arm bones, which in turn are supported by the leg bones. This eliminates the tensing of the abdominal and lower back muscles which would have to hold the upper body steady if it was in a more upright position. This also helps you automatically drop right back into your position after the recoil pulse.

Another principle is called "shooting against your ligaments." This means orienting some part of your body's support structure so that you get gravity to move it to its natural limit of joint motion, where it can't move any further, and will stay put by your own weight without using much, if any, muscle tension. As I cover each position in following chapters, I will discuss how these principles best apply.

It is important to note that your zero may vary slightly from one position to

NRA highpower bullseye is very challenging position shooting. No help from the sling allowed in stage 1 standing. The stiff shooting coat helps, but correct position is everything. The ten-ring is seven inches across, 200 yards away.

Same target as standing, for stage 2 rapid-fire from sitting or kneeling. Cross-ankle sitting shown here; note aggressive forward lean of upper body. 1907 loop sling, padded mitt and jacket, and cheek-to-thumb weld all help.

Stage three is prone rapid-fire at 300 yards. The ten-ring is still seven inches across. Stage four is slow-fire prone at 600 yards, with a ten-ring of twelve inches diameter.

the next, mostly as a reaction to how your body moves differently under recoil in different positions. Even small changes within a given position, such as how the support hand holds the fore-end or how the face contacts the stock, can make a difference, so learn to be consistent with every detail of each position. Once you are happy with your shooting in multiple positions, you can fire for zero comparison. Obviously this will really only apply to those positions that are so steady as to allow the shooting of a tight group, such as sitting with a loop sling, prone with the loop sling, and either with some sort of rest, but it is still worthwhile to explore.

Last, remember that, as a general rule, the closer you get to the ground the steadier you will be.

You may find that getting into position is difficult, to say the least. If you are young, slim, and limber, it should be no problem. If you are overweight, inflexible, or just plain not-young-anymore, you will probably find yourself struggling in certain positions and perhaps yelping in pain here and there. Don't force your body to do anything it doesn't want to do, or you'll wind up stretching a muscle or ligament to the tearing point. Go gently and see just what your capabilities and limitations are. A program of regular gentle total-body stretching will work wonders, as will regular exercise and getting your waistline down to where you always wished it was.

The sitting position is a particular sore point in regards to getting a good forward lean; you may have to adopt a more upright version until your waist slims down a bit and your lower back muscles become more flexible. In prone, the mus-

cles behind your support-side shoulder will object loudly to getting your support arm elbow properly under the rifle. If you cannot get a textbook-perfect position, do the best you can to follow the principles involved as far as your body will let you. The longer you practice these positions, the easier they will become.

NATURAL POINT OF AIM

In any position, the arrangement of your relaxed body combines to point the rifle muzzle naturally at some spot. If you were to assume a position, close your eyes, relax as much as possible letting the rifle point where it may, inhale, exhale, hold your breath, keep relaxed, open your eyes, and look through the sights without disturbing your aim, this is your NPA. The rifle will always want to point there for that position. Having your NPA and target coincide means the rifle will want to point there, allowing you to relax as much as possible, resulting in the steadiest hold. Using NPA lets your position do all the hard work for you. Effortless aiming.

If your NPA does not coincide with your target, trying to shove the rifle away from your NPA towards your target will result in a battle between your hands and the rest of your body. This results in excess muscle tension and a conflicting, unstable position. With the exception of the snap shot and to a lesser extent the standing position, never aim the rifle by pushing it on target with your hands!

To get the two to coincide, arrange your shooting position so that the horizontal orientation of your entire body naturally aligns the rifle on the target in windage (side-to-side), and support your

You're in position, but did you align your natural point of aim on target?

limbs in such a way as to achieve the correct elevation. Always check it by closing your eyes, relaxing, and opening your eyes to see where your rifle is aimed. Adjust your body until you are as close to coincidence as possible. With practice, it will take only a few seconds and you will learn to assume position closer and closer to target/NPA coincidence. I will go into detail on how to adjust your horizontal and vertical NPA for each position as I cover them later.

One important detail to keep in mind about setting your NPA on target: set your elevation when your lungs are empty at that natural respiratory pause. That way, when you are doing the inhale/exhale/pause cycle, with intent to shoot at the pause after the exhale, your sights (which will move as you inhale/exhale) will be right on target at the same time you will want to press the trigger. Thus your breathing, trigger pull, and NPA will all be in sync, which makes hitting a lot easier.

Once you have settled into position, get into the habit of always testing your NPA by doing the close-eyes-relax-open-eyes test. Your natural point-of-aim can also be evaluated while you are shooting by letting the rifle find its own position after recoil and seeing where the sight settles. Thus you have two techniques to tell you if your NPA is right. The first is something you can dry practice in your living room, so make sure you put some time into it. It's a great way to learn and remember your best position. Put up an aiming point (I use a black thumbtack on the wall) and see how steadily you can hold on it. Figure all this out at home then test it on the range in practice. Cor-

rect use of NPA will do wonders for your shooting, make you consistent from day to day on the range, and cure a lot of those "what the heck happened" shots. It really does all the hard work for you.

The effect of this concept can be witnessed by taking a position (say, sitting with the sling) and settling in with the rifle pointing to its NPA in a good relaxed position with a snug sling. Observe the wobble zone of your sight. Next, push the rifle over sideways with your hands ten or fifteen degrees to a new aimpoint, without shifting your position, and try to hold it there. Observe the wobble of your sight in this situation. Odds are the relaxed NPA position will have a smaller wobble zone and will also allow you to hold it longer without the wobble getting worse.

NPA, a correct shooting position, and a shooting loop sling really do all the hard work for you. The stability you can achieve is almost astounding. With a good sitting position and a loop sling, you should be able to achieve a "wobble zone" of your crosshairs of three minutes of angle, while completely relaxed, and be able to hold this position for many minutes without undue strain, and get your shot off within the inner two of those three minutes of angle. That means shooting about a four-inch group at 200 yards from sitting! You can actually start to doze off in such a position and (due to the loop sling) the rifle will not waver off the target. No, I'm not kidding.

Natural point-of-aim is not only key to a quick hit from a steady position, it helps you plant a rapid follow-up shot as well. With it, the rifle will come down from recoil all by itself right onto a near-perfect hold on your target. This allows you to concentrate only on firing the next shot. An unnatural point of aim results in the rifle coming back from recoil pointed at wherever your NPA actually is, requiring you to (incorrectly) muscle it back on target for every shot, or (correctly) shift your NPA onto your target. So, when you fire a shot, follow through by watching your sights as the gun recovers from recoil. It will tell you a lot about your position. You will know you are doing it right when you can close your eyes, relax completely, sag forward into the buttstock (which tightens up the sling), open your eyes while still relaxed, and see your sight sitting exactly where you would have it to fire without you doing any work to hold it there.

When you get this right, your front

Aggressive forward lean of upper body plants its weight on arm bones, supported by leg bones, eliminating muscle use by using gravity instead. Support arm bones directly under rifle resting on leg, and loop sling use holds up rifle instead of arm muscle. If my NPA is on target, I can fall asleep here and the rifle will not waver off the target. Really. (In fact, I think I was dozing for this one.)

Apply good position principles even when using what help nature provides.

sight will seem to find the target all by itself, it will want to stay there, your sight picture will magically reproduce itself after recoil, and it will seem like you are just along for the ride. If you are shooting a string of rapid fire shots at a single target, as in highpower bullseye, correct NPA is crucial to getting good hits within the time limits. Relax, inhale, exhale, pause, press...BOOM, follow through. Relax, inhale, exhale, pause, press.... BOOM, follow through. With normal breathing you can fire a controlled, aimed shot every 3-4 seconds, with your

Log and pack rest, but still using loop sling and aggressive forward lean.

front sight falling right back to its aim-point by itself. This is called "Rifleman's Cadence": aimed, controlled rapid fire. For a hunter, it allows a fast second shot if necessary. When you can see this happen, it's a really big "Aha!" moment.

When developing your shooting positions, what you are trying to achieve is, first, getting your position correct, second, getting your NPA to coincide with your aiming point, and third, learning to get both of these things simultaneously and as fast as possible. This allows you to hit anything you can see within reasonable range within a matter of a few seconds.

Remember as you practice that movements you ultimately want to perform quickly should be learned slowly. Slowness makes for learning correctly, and also allows you to work for smoothness and economy of motion. Smoothness and economy of the correct motion result in speed without sacrificing accuracy. The right process gives you the desired end result.

When learning the various positions on the range, you usually have the luxury of a nice flat level surface with which to work, allowing you to construct "target range" correct positions. In the field, however, you will find that tilted or lumpy ground, rocks, brush, tall grass, and even less fun things (thornbush, small cactus, red ants, and the odd rattlesnake or scorpion) will complicate matters considerably. The key here is to stick to the essentials of the position as best you can while adapting to the terrain. Try to maintain skeletal support and desirable weight distribution (usually forward lean), NPA, and other key elements of that particular position as best you can. If you find you cannot, then it is wise (if circumstances allow) to either try a different shooting position or move to a better location. This applies to pure position shooting as well as using some sort of mechanical rest (bipod, sticks, etc.) or field-expedient natural rest (log, rock, etc.).

Always remember exactly what you are trying to do when creating a particular position; don't just flop onto the ground and squirm around (especially when there are cactus and red ants around – ouchouchouch). Keeping the principles of correct position firmly in mind at all times will be an enormous help when terrain prevents you from creating a textbook position. Make this concept a full-time part of your "rifleshooter's mindset" and it will allow you to get very steady very fast under all but the most inhospitable of conditions. And remember to relax your mind as well as your body.

Starting from standing position, you should (if you are reasonably limber) eventually be able to assume sitting with a sling and hit (every time) a paper plate (or that 8-inch smallbore target) at 200 yards in no more than ten or twelve seconds and perhaps quite a bit less; standing to prone with sling, same target at 300 yards, no more than 12-15 seconds, and possibly less than 10. It will certainly take some time in practice to sort all this out, but this is the goal you should be keeping in mind as you train. It is achievable with the triad of NPA, correct position, and a shooting loop sling. Now, let's look at what a shooting loop sling is and how it works, and then go on to the individual positions.

CHAPTER 8

THE SHOOTING LOOP SLING

One of the most useful rifle shooting aids is also one of the most neglected. That is the use of the loop sling. The support and steadiness it provides, when properly used, is enormous. Learning this proper use is extremely important if you wish to reach your full potential. Contrary to what you may have read before, the sling does not "tie the rifle to your shoulder," or to your arm for that matter. What it does is to replace your support arm bicep muscle in holding up the weight of the rifle, not only taking one more trembling muscle out of the picture, but also preventing the support arm elbow joint angle from opening up and lowering the rifle, and even helping support the weight of the upper body in certain positions.

While proper use of the shooting loop sling was long a staple of military training and was well known amongst hunters, the military started getting away from teaching it in the years after the Korean War. As a result, the knowledge of how to use this handy technique has all but disappeared from both the military and civilian worlds of riflery. This is a shame, as a properly set-up sling is a major aid to gaining a steady position. Col. Cooper's observations, if I recall correctly, were that the shooting loop sling is useful in perhaps 60% of rifle hunting situations, and increases your steadiness by about 30%. I personally think he was being conservative.

The best use of the shooting loop sling requires the support arm elbow (left elbow if you shoot righty) to be rested on a support. This can be a log, car hood (if legal for hunting in your state – it's not in mine!), the ground (in prone), or your own leg (kneeling, squatting, or sitting). When your elbow is hanging in the air you still have to use your support-side shoulder (front deltoid) muscle to hold everything up, so much of the steadiness a loop sling affords is wasted, since the only muscle it replaces is the bicep. If your elbow is not supported you can't truly relax your support arm from shoulder to fingertips.

If the situation calls for – and allows – the taking of any position or rest where the support arm elbow is planted on something solid, the shooting sling is the quickest, simplest, and least cumbersome steadiness aid there is. Got a bipod? Fine. How much weight does it add to your rifle, and how long does it take to deploy it and adjust its length properly? Carrying shooting sticks? Okay, how do you like carrying them all day? How much movement do you make setting them up

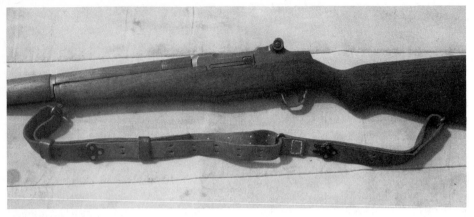

The USGI M1907 leather loop sling, on the mighty M1 rifle.

properly? Granted, if your hunting style is to sit down, set up, and not move all day, the aforementioned shooting aids will work quite well. But if handiness and speed of deployment count, it's hard to beat the right kind of shooting sling. With the modern fast-acquisition loop sling you can loop up in it while moving into position.

A proper shooting loop sling (as distinct from just a carry strap), used in the right situation, supports the weight of the rifle and allows you to relax into your position, thus freeing your muscles of the strain of holding up the rifle and recovering it on target after every shot. The rested elbow relieves your shoulder muscles of the task of holding up both arm and rifle. Once your shoulder is no longer doing the work, the task of holding up the rifle is left to your support arm bicep, which has to keep tense to keep the weight of the rifle from sagging downwards. Now, wouldn't it be nice to be able to substitute yet another stable support for a muscle that can tire and tremble?

The shooting sling performs this task very nicely by forming a loop, which wraps around the back of your upper support arm (the higher the better) and the front of your wrist. This loop captures and surrounds your entire arm, from the armpit to wrist, preventing the elbow joint from moving in a more open direction. Viewed from the side, you have a point-downwards rigid triangle formed by the sling horizontal across the top, and your forearm and upper arm forming the other two sides.

Gravity, attempting to pull the rifle downwards, has a tendency to work against your bicep muscle, making your support arm want to open up its angle through movement of the elbow joint (if your support elbow is positioned directly under the rifle). But the sling, by wrapping around both your support wrist and support upper arm, will start to tighten up if this happens. Forward and downward motion of that wrist against the sling pulls the sling against the back of your upper arm, and once it tightens up it will prevent your support wrist from moving any further downward (where the weight of the rifle wants to push it). Your bones and the sling do all the work.

A Savage 99, sporting an early type speed loop sling called the CW sling, now supplanted by the superior Ching sling.

Again, it is critical to have your support elbow placed directly under the rifle in your shooting position. If it is off to the outside, gravity will tend to pull the rifle downwards with a sideways direction, toward the trigger hand side. This is a shoulder joint motion, which the sling will not prevent. Remember to have your shooting position built with the support elbow as directly under the rifle as your flexibility will allow.

The total length of the loop section must be set to your own arm length and body size. Remember that when I use the term "tight" I am not referring to how tightly the loop circles your upper arm, but how short the loop is and how tightly it brings the rifle butt back into your shoulder. As a general rule, the bigger you are, the longer the loop needs to be. If the loop is too long, relaxing your support arm until the sling tightens up will result in the rifle muzzle pointing too low, and without the necessary tension to give stability. If the loop is too short, you will not be able to get your support forearm to move forward far enough to get the buttstock into your shoulder.

The correct length of the loop is critical. It should be just long enough to let the rifle move forward enough to barely get its buttstock into your shoulder (without a big struggle) with the clothes you will be wearing while hunting. This creates sufficient tension in the sling loop straps to allow it to do its work well. Basically the rifle is "wedged" in place under firm pressure, with the rearward motion limit being the butt in your shoulder, and the forward motion limit being the back of the sling loop where it wraps around the back of your upper arm. If the sling loop is even slightly too long, you will end up using bicep muscle to do some of the work of holding up the rifle, and you lose some of the steadiness and ability to relax into position that a shorter loop and more snug "wedge" fit of the rifle affords you.

When you set your loop length correctly, there should be a definite feeling of the sling strap biting deep into the back of your upper support arm and the rifle buttstock being pretty firmly jammed against your shoulder – but, it should not take a fight to get it placed there. Anything less snug will not give you the ultimate support available. You may find that you need about an inch or so more length in prone than in sitting. And if you set the length while wearing a t-shirt, you'll need to add an inch or two for winter clothing.

The higher the sling loop is on your upper support arm, the better leverage it has to give support, the tighter the rifle butt will be in your shoulder, and (for a given loop length) the smaller the angle will be between upper and lower support arm (across the elbow joint), which has the effect of keeping your support hand (and rifle) higher. Now if the sling loop starts to slide down your upper arm, it will have the same effect as if you lengthened the loop, allowing your support hand (and rifle) to droop lower and reducing the snugness of the buttstock in your shoulder. This is generally a less stable condition, but under certain situations while taking a shot in the field, the fit of sling loop and buttstock snugness and/or rifle height can be 'fudged' slightly by raising or lowering the sling loop on your upper support arm to fit the immediate needs of the position. This is something to keep in mind when in the field, but when first starting to experiment with the sling at home and on the range, always start your sling loop position and loop length adjustment at the 'high and too tight' and fine-tune from there.

This concept is extremely important in obtaining the full potential of the sling. When you first adjust the loop length of your sling, you MUST adjust it to be too short to get the rifle butt into your shoulder for that position, then adjust it longer one hole at a time, checking to see if you can barely get the butt to wedge tightly against your shoulder. For that position and the thickness of clothing worn, that is the most advantageous loop length for maximum support. If you do not do this, you will not be able to judge whether or not the sling is really at its best loop length adjustment. Going to a too-short-to-use loop length is what gives you a baseline to measure just how much longer the best length is in relation to the too-short length. Without doing this you will not know where you are in the loop length spectrum and may not realize that you can significantly improve matters by going tighter. How much tighter? Until it can't be done, then back off slightly until it can!

A good test is to get into prone or sitting position, then take your trigger hand off the rifle. If the butt-stock drops from your shoulder you are probably too long and loose in the loop length.

If you are using the sitting or kneeling position, an important side effect of its support is to allow you to naturally fall back into your relaxed position after the rifle finishes recoiling – if you are leaning well into the rifle with your upper body weight biased forward. This is important in that it allows fast, automatic recovery from recoil right back to target alignment, with little or no effort by you. And with this forward-leaning position, you can actually have the sling support

Remington Model 7 .243, with home-made Ching sling.

much of your upper body weight. By leaning your chest and shoulders well into the rifle butt, you push the rifle forwards, which pulls the sling forward with it, which automatically causes the loop to tighten against the back of your support arm to its maximum. If you have enough of a forward lean in your position, so that total relaxation would tend to make your upper body fall forwards rather than backwards, you can essentially "lean against the sling." This means you can sit there all day in a relaxed state without actually holding either the rifle up with your arm or shoulder muscles (if your support elbow is solidly rested on something) or holding up your upper body with your back or stomach muscles. This concept is extremely important, especially in sitting; give it careful consideration in every position that you develop that uses the sling.

You can learn to use the combination of shooting sling and proper position principles with surprising speed and steadiness. This combination, properly learned and performed, will allow you (if you are reasonably limber!) to go from standing ready,

to dropping into sitting while putting your arm through the sling before hitting the ground, and getting that hit on a 10-inch circle at 200 yards with rock-solid steadiness in a total time of ten or twelve seconds – and possibly less – with a fully relaxed position and a "wobble zone" of your crosshairs that should stay well within the target zone.

In contrast to the shooting loop sling, we have the basic carrying strap sling, which is often used as a "hasty sling" for

A very skilled young lady, with her CZ .22 rimfire equipped with a USGI M1 web sling. This girl outshot a US Army sniper at a recent Appleseed marksmanship clinic! Her pink hat says, "Shoot like a girl if you can."

Hasty-hasty. With a twist of your wrists, flick the sling up under your support elbow.

The hasty-hasty in standing.

shooting. Let's reiterate: a proper shooting sling takes over from the bicep muscle, and it does this by looping from the front swivel, around your wrist, then to the rear around the back of your support upper arm, then wrapping forward again to create the loop. It is this loop that creates the rigid triangle of upper arm, forearm, and sling strap. The carry strap used in "hasty" mode does not wrap forward again; instead it continues on towards the rear swivel at the buttstock. As such, it neither replaces the bicep muscle nor holds up the weight of the rifle, since it does not loop around and capture both upper and lower arms.

With a carry strap used in "hasty" mode, you can get into it (through, around, and through again) very quickly, and will gain a slight degree of steadiness, but your bicep is still doing the work and can still allow the rifle to sag

downwards – something a proper loop sling totally prevents. And forget about "leaning against the sling" with a carry strap. All the hasty does is dampen tremors in your arm. The best use of hasty is in the standing position since it is quite quick, and does provide some support. If you make the sling short enough that the rear part of it is draped tautly across the shooter's chest, it takes up some of the weight of the rifle. The hasty works well for a quick offhand shot or for when you have a military 1907 or web sling (described below) but don't have time to get into the loop.

One variant of the hasty is the "hasty-hasty." This is simply having the strap hook under your support elbow when in the standing position. You do not wrap your support hand around the sling as in hasty or loop, but simply flick or rock your wrists while holding the rifle so as to swing the hanging strap under your elbow and brace it there. It is eyeblink-quick to acquire and offers a smidge more support than just holding up the rifle with muscle.

There are four basic kinds of shooting loop sling commonly available:

- the traditional military M1907 leather loop sling, with its double metal prongs fitting double holes;
- the military cotton web sling, introduced after WWII as a replacement for the M1907;
- the two-piece target shooter's sling and cuff; and
- the modern Ching sling.

The military type slings are extremely steady and can be adjusted to fit perfectly for any given person's body size and shooting position. They also work as a carrying strap.

MILITARY LEATHER LOOP SLING

With the M1907, you grasp the rearwards part of the forward loop section and twist it a half turn, the strap closest to the rifle moving towards the support arm. Then thrust your arm through the rearwards part of the forward loop and close it around your upper arm with the leather keeper loops. Ideally you will have a keeper on either side of the brass double-prong (called a "frog"). The frog, plugged into a set of double holes, is what you adjust to set the loop length. You can slide the strap around your arm so that the frog cinches up against the keeper in front of your bicep, tightening the sling around your arm, then slide the other keeper up against the frog. This is how you'd tighten the sling on a target range, for spending extended periods of time in position. In the field you can just keep the loop loose around your arm without

4 loop sling types. From top: Ching, M1907, GI web, 2-piece target sling & cuff.

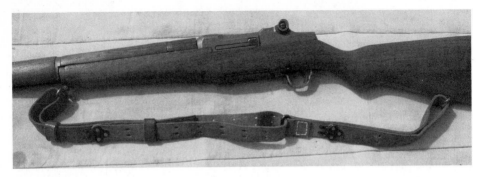

The M1907 installed on an M1. Note the forward part is the loop.

cinching it down, since the tension in the sling loop will hold it against your arm for the few seconds you will need to be in position. Then wrap your arm down and around the sling and thrust your hand between sling and rifle to place it on the fore-end up against the sling swivel in a relaxed, wedged position.

I have recently found a way to get into the M1907 fairly quickly. The method described above can take eight or ten seconds, or longer if the sling is stiff and you are not well-practiced with it. I find that if I run the frog and keepers forward up against the front swivel, leaving the loop as open as possible, and with the front loop adjusted to be shortened all the way, I can grab the rearmost part of the forward loop section with my trigger hand, pull it under my support elbow, and up my upper support arm to a workable position. Then I re-grip the pistol

M1907: The arm hole in the loop, with half turn twisted loop.

Insert support arm through loop.

Slide loop all the way up support upper arm.

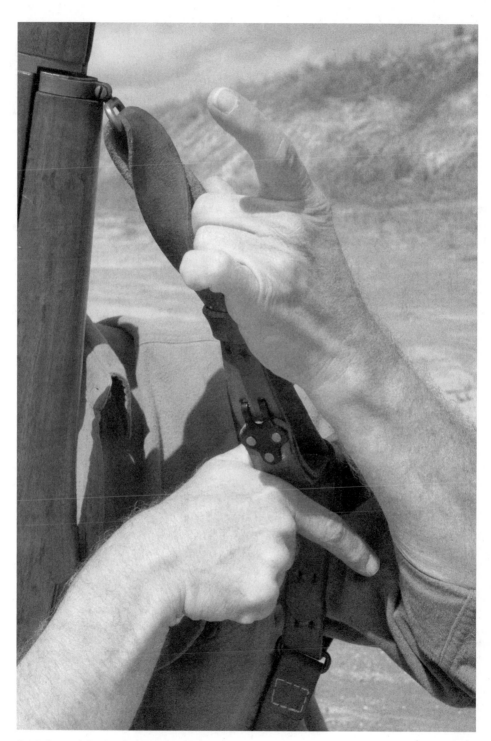

Rotate loop to bring frog and keeper to bicep.

Cinch keeper/frog/keeper to lock it tight.

grip with my trigger hand, having always maintained my forward support hand grip. This movement can be done very quickly, while dropping into kneeling or squatting. It is important to keep a firm grip with the support hand to maintain sling tension. This method works very well for a "hasty loop", without wrapping your support hand around the sling or cinching it down tight around your upper support arm. It provides some support, but trades maximum support for speed.

For more support at the cost of a couple more seconds, after I get to the above sling situation, I let go with the front hand, and push my front hand/forearm through the loop and wrap it around the sling in the normal fashion and jam it up against the front swivel. No cinching-down tightening of the loop around

my arm is done. I can do this while going from standing to aiming in kneeling in about four seconds flat, sitting about 6-7 seconds. Much faster than the classic method of looping up and cinching down. If you can adjust the sling short enough to be tight for your build, it offers good loop support.

This method gets the loop on your upper arm very fast, but has some issues. I have to have the front loop set to minimum length, unworkable for conventional use. However, it gives me a quick acquisition and a workable though un-cinched loop, and if I have time for a deliberate shot, I can always re-set the loop length and use it in the normal fashion. The forward hand is wrapped around the sling and wedged against the front swivel in the usual securely trapped fashion, so this is more stable

In sitting position with support forearm wrapped around sling and hand between sling and stock and wedged against front swivel.

Hasty sling: arm goes between sling and rifle.

Hasty sling: arm then wraps around sling.

Hasty sling: hand then goes between sling and rifle.

The hasty sling in offhand. Note rear strap across chest.

than simply gripping the stock, though about two seconds slower.

Practical speed points to ponder: for a relatively easy target and a quick shot (say a deer inside 150 yds from squatting/kneeling), simply keep gripping the fore-end with the forward hand and pull the loop up on the upper support arm, without pushing the forward hand through the loop and wrapping it around the straps. This is very fast though the least steady.

For a somewhat more demanding shot that still requires speed, one can add the forward hand pushing through the loop and wrapping around, costing about two more seconds but adding more stability.

For a shot where time is not of the essence and maximum support is required, you can re-adjust the sling for conventional cinched-down use.

None of this comes close to the one-second loop-up of the Ching, but it does add some interesting speed flexibility to the old classic.

GI GREEN COTTON OR NYLON WEB SLING

The GI green cotton or nylon web sling is somewhat different. The detachable sheet metal hook goes to the buttstock swivel, and the other end of the sling is threaded through the front swivel. For hasty or hasty-hasty use, the rear hook stays attached to the rear swivel. For loop use, you detach the rear sling hook from the rear rifle swivel. Just above the rear hook will be a rectangular black metal buckle. There will be a pass of sling strap across the center of the buckle. Grasp this and pull it out to make the loop through which you put your support arm (don't forget the half twist). The lever clamp buckle near the forward

For the speed application of the 1907 sling, set the frog to make the loop as short as possible, and run it and the keepers to the front sling swivel, to maximize the open area of the front loop section of sling.

From the ready position, grab the rear of the front loop section with you trigger hand, where the rear section of sling attaches. Keep hold of the rifle fore-end with the support hand throughout these moves.

Pull the rear of the loop section up onto your support arm, high as you can, pushing forward on the rifle to pull the loop snug against the back of your arm.

You are dropping into position as you loop up. Note that the support arm is fully surrounded by both sides of the sling loop, and the support hand has maintained its grip, without wrapping around the straps. Ready for a quick, loop-sling-supported shot.

Once you are in position, you can also push your support hand through the loop...

...so as to wrap it around the sling straps in the usual fashion...

...and place it up against the front swivel...

...for more support and a relaxed support hand. The cost in time is only two or three seconds more.

The GI web sling. Note metal camlock and metal buckle.

Remove hook from rear swivel.

The strap through the buckle becomes the loop.

Pull out web strap from the buckle center to make loop.

Half twist front loop and insert support arm through loop to above bicep. Metal hook to outside of arm means your half twist was in correct direction.

In sitting position with support forearm wrapped around sling and hand between sling and stock and wedged against front swivel, with metal hook to outside of arm.

part of the sling is loosened to adjust the length of the sling from the support arm loop to the front swivel, which is the loop length, then tightened down.

For use on a target range, or for deliberate hunting such as sitting for long periods of time or crawling up on a distant pronghorn antelope where reaction time is not an issue, they will do. But with loop-up taking eight to ten seconds, we can do better.

TWO-PIECE TARGET SLING AND CUFF

The two-piece target sling and cuff are specialized pieces of equipment, and require one to wear a heavy cuff with a D-ring on one's arm, and hook the end of the sling strap into it. It cannot double as a carry strap.

THE CHING SLING

Designed by Eric Ching, the Ching sling was designed to remedy the faults of all of the above slings. It provides the muscle-replacement loop of the military and target slings, operates with exactly the same motion (and speed) of the carry strap used in "hasty" mode, and still doubles as a carry strap! The Ching sling looks exactly like a simple carry strap with one important addition: a short section of strap which is anchored in an extra swivel at the rear of the fore-end just ahead of the action floorplate, and whose other end terminates in a rectangular metal loop which slides freely along the middle of the main strap. It is this short strap that allows the formation of the shooting loop. This requires a total of three swivel stud placements on

Vertical view of the Ching sling.

Horizontal view of the Ching sling. The area forward of the short center strap is where you insert your arm to make the loop. Note the half twist at the front.

your rifle stock, so you will have to add one to the pair that probably came from the factory.

The Ching is applied to your arm in the same motion as the "hasty sling" use of the carry strap. With rifle held horizontal by the trigger hand, the support hand passes between the forward part of the hanging sling loop (ahead of the separate short strap) and the rifle fore-end, with your arm going through as far up to the armpit as possible. Then the support hand moves downwards, below the sling strap, back around to the near side of it, then upwards, and then you pass it back through between the sling and stock again just a short distance, just enough to be able to get your support hand under the fore-end in a normal firing position (do not grip the fore-end, just wedge your open relaxed hand against the sling swivel).

Essentially, you are simply just wrapping your arm around the sling, with the sling touching you by wrapping around the side of your wrist and the back of your upper arm. The short strap section pulls against the main strap in the region of your upper arm on the inside, comes to a stop against a loop-length-adjusting stop button on the main strap, and is pulled tight against its swivel stud, forming the shooting loop.

The loop length on a Ching sling is set by a little stop button affixed to the main strap in one of a series of adjustment holes, against which the sliding brass hoop of the short strap comes to rest. Simply assume the desired position with the rifle and sling, and set the stop button in the hole that gives you just the right length. If the butt goes into your shoulder snugly without a struggle, and if the rifle

Insert support arm into Ching sling forward loop.

Wrap support arm around sling.

Insert support hand between sling and stock and wedge it against the swivel.

In standing firing position.

is held up by the sling at the appropriate height, you're set. As stated above, you may find that you need about an inch or so more length in prone than in sitting. And if you set the length while wearing a t-shirt, you'll need to add an inch or two for winter clothing.

When install your Ching, add a half-twist clockwise (when looking down at the front swivel) to the front end of the strap when you attach it. This half-twist will allow the sling to lay flat against your wrist as it wraps around it, instead of having its edge bite into your arm. This clockwise twist direction is for right-handers; left-handers should use the opposite direction.

For a hunter, a quickly-assumed, rock-steady "slung" position ought to be at the top of your bag of tricks. So, how do we use the Ching to help attain this?

First, put your arm in the sling as you go from standing ready to whatever position you have selected. You should be in the sling by the time you hit the position. Second, make sure your support elbow is as directly under the rifle as possible (with any type of loop sling). Avoid positions where that elbow is well to the outside of the rifle. The reason is that the sling only works to hold up the rifle if gravity pulls the rifle in a direction that would cause the opening of your elbow joint angle (what the sling loop prevents). This is what happens when your elbow is under the rifle. If it's off to the outside, gravity does not work directly against your elbow. Instead, there is a tendency for the rifle to fall sideways away from your support arm toward the trigger hand side. This produces a sideways pivot of your support arm, flexing from the shoulder and pivoting over the elbow point, identical to the motion you try to make in arm-wrestling. Your support arm tilts over sideways with the elbow joint angle remaining unchanged.

The sling has no control over this type of motion. Thus, the rifle will tend to fall sideways (rightwards for a right-hander) and also forward off of your shoulder, especially after recoil. This works exactly the same way in prone, so make sure you understand this principle and apply it to all sling use where the elbow is rested on something solid. This may cause some pain in the muscles behind your shoulder until they get used to being stretched that far (just ignore those people who claim the sling is an infernal torture instrument designed by evil sadists!). And make sure you lean as far forward in your position as physically possible, so your upper body can rest itself against the sling.

One caveat: use of a shooting sling will put some stress on the fore-end of your rifle, and may influence the barrel enough to cause a change in your zero, if you got your zero from a benchrest.. The way I deal with this is to assume that any shot that is long will require the sling, and any shot that is taken without the sling will probably be very close (say, from standing at 25-75 yards). Therefore, I zero my rifles from sitting using the loop sling, and figure that at close range without the sling (say, a standing shot at 50 yards), any difference in zero due to not using the sling will not matter at all. From 100 yards on out, I'll be loop-slung and shooting from squatting, kneeling, sitting, or prone – and my zero will be on at these longer ranges. And you can apply the sling even when shooting from a

Slam your support arm through the Ching loop as you start down into position!

Support hand gets around sling and back onto fore-end while still dropping into position...

...freeing the trigger hand to brace your impact against the ground.

Standing to shooting from slung sitting, in less than ten seconds.

rest. If your rifle has a free-floated barrel, there should be no issue with this.

The end result of proper Ching sling use is a quickly-attained, stable position allowing nearly complete relaxation, little or no muscle effort, and the ability to quickly recover from recoil. This result is definitely worth the initial effort. You may find that with sufficient development, practice, and proper sling use, a good sitting position using a loop sling is steady enough to hit a saucer at 250 yards – and it's attainable from standing ready in a few seconds.

An interesting capability of the Ching sling I just recently discovered is to help hold a heavy rifle up in the standard ready position for long periods of time while still-hunting through the woods. On a recent elk hunt, by using the hasty-hasty position of the main strap under my support elbow while in the ready position, I was able to hold up my heavy .35 Whelen bolt rifle for long periods of time with hardly any effort at all, due to the loop configuration of the Ching. A very happy discovery! And, you can quickly mount the rifle this way maintaining the hasty-hasty sling mode support!

As mentioned in the previous chapter on position and NPA, the combination of a correct and appropriate position, a tight loop sling, and having your NPA coincide with your aiming point will let you relax into position with a wobble zone inside your desired hit zone. This totally eliminates the common condition of having your sight weaving on and off your aim point which causes the temptation to yank the trigger when the sight crosses your aim point. Instead it lets you get off a nice surprise trigger break while the sight

hangs right where you want it. This last bit on easy trigger management is extremely important, since the weave-and-yank condition is a big cause of missing (and flinching!) for most shooters. Getting rid of this is a big, big deal folks.

Having used the M1907 military sling on an M1 Garand rifle to shoot high-power rifle bullseye competition from the sitting position at 200 yards in rapid fire, prone at 300 yards in rapid fire, and prone at 600 yards in slow fire, and having used the Ching on my .270 bolt gun in Col. Cooper's General Rifle course, I have a great deal of respect for what a properly used sling can do, and I see no need of either bipod or shooting sticks for most of the types of field shooting I do. The one exception is calling coyotes, where having the rifle in shooting position for twenty minutes at a time with trigger hand in position while having the off hand free to hold the mouth call makes a bipod or sticks an attractive alternative. Not that I have actually gotten around to using them yet, though…

You can mess around with the M1907 or GI web if you like, or if you absolutely refuse to install another swivel stud on Ol' Betsy. You may, as I still do, even currently have one or two on your rifles. They are a good setup and rock-steady when you are properly in them (you might want to compare your installation to the photos; it is amazing how often they are put on wrong), but my advice is to put a Ching sling on your hunting rifle. Period. The advantage in speed and versatility it gives you is simply phenomenal. It is the use of the Ching that will allow you to reach your highest potential for speed with accuracy.

Ready position with the Ching sling already in hasty-hasty mode. This helps support weight of rifle when still-hunting all day. Note that forward support hand is not wrapped around sling.

My elk thumper: Mauser 98 in .35 Whelen Improved, with half-octagon barrel, Leupold 1.75x-6x scope, California English wood, and Ching sling on flush-mount studs.

MAKING YOUR OWN CHING SLING

And for those on a budget, well, if you are patient, careful, handy with a razor blade and drill gun, and can measure, you can make a Ching sling yourself in a couple of hours or less with about ten or twelve bucks spent at your local leather store and an extra set of sling swivels and studs.

Get a leather strip the width of your sling swivel inner width about 50-52 inches long and about 1/10- to 1/8-inch thick. Tandy often sells such strips premade in set widths including 1- and 1¼-inch and lengths varying by the foot (get the five foot rather than the four, as it is a bit tight). Also, a package of Chicago screws of a length (the shorter ones) that will allow two thicknesses of the leather strip to be screwed together, a rectangular brass or steel hoop large enough to let two (but not three!) layers of the leather strip slide through it easily, then hit the hardware store. Obtain a package of black rubber faucet washers about the diameter of the width of the leather strap (slightly smaller is OK but wider looks bad) and with a hole just large enough to let the Chicago screw nut end body go through (a smaller hole is OK but not a way bigger one!), and a drill that will make that same size hole (7/32-inch) that will let the Chicago nut female body pass through easily but not loosely. You may already these things at home. Also, while the drill may be necessary for the hole in the faucet washer, you can also use a punch of 3/16-inch commonly sold in leathercraft stores to use on the leather strap.

Cut a piece about 11.5 to 12 inches (no longer) from the strap. Dress off the ends neatly (square, round, your desire), and fold the end over about 1.5 inches or so, in such a fashion that the rough side of the leather faces itself inside the fold. Wetting the leather thoroughly helps make a tight fold. Start the drill through the end piece about ½ inch back from the tip, centered for width, and go right

Flush-mount studs are easier on your hands.

These use twist-and-lock T-head swivels.

through both layers. Put your metal hoop in place and screw the strap end together (you may want to wait until the leather is dry to avoid metal corrosion). At the other end repeat but use your third sling swivel when assembling. You now have the center strap complete.

With the remains of the long strap, do the same thing to the ends as you did with the short strap, for your existing pair of swivels. Do not yet assemble. From one end of the main strap, carefully mark a series of spots for holes to be cut, on the centerline for width and either one or ¾ inch apart. These will be the adjustment holes for both the main strap and the short strap. Run them all the way from the one end hole for about two-thirds the length of the main strap. These will be the holes that the butt end of the main sling strap will fold over onto for its overall length adjustment, and also for the stop adjustment for the short strap shooting loop length. Drill or punch them as neatly as possible from the smooth side of the leather with the 7/32-inch size punch or drill that allows a Chicago screw nut body to pass through easily. Bear in mind that the end of the main strap where you started drilling these holes is the butt or rear end of the sling. Also grab one of the washers and ream out its hole to fit the Chicago screw nut if necessary.

Now, before you screw together the main strap ends, slide the hoop of the short strap onto the main strap so that the short strap is on the rough side of the main strap. Which way the rough faces on the short strap is immaterial, but I have it facing the forward end of the sling. Screw the ends of the main straps over onto your existing swivels. One last step is necessary: screw the washer (now our stop button) onto the main strap, on the smooth side of the leather, in one of the holes in about the center of the main strap. Make sure the washer stop button is installed to the rear of the metal hoop of the short strap. You are now ready for installation (once you get the third swivel installed on your rifle's fore-end, about ¾ inch in front of the bottom metal). The end of the main strap with all the holes goes to the buttstock, leather smooth side out away from the rifle. Please refer back to the instructions referenced earlier about the half-twist at the front swivel. And don't forget to oil the sling moderately well, especially at the folds around the hoop and swivels.

Once you can try getting into the sling in position, you will find out where that stop button should be. If you can't even get the butt into your shoulder, or have to struggle to do so, the loop is too short, which means the stop button should be moved to the rear. If you can get the butt into your shoulder easily but when you relax your support arm and let the rifle sag until the sling tightens up the rifle points too low, your loop is too long. You have to move the stop button forwards to shorten the loop, which will raise up the rifle. The key feeling is "very snug, verging on tight, but without a fight," which of course will depend on the amount of clothes you are wearing at that time. Thicker clothing requires more loop length for the same feeling as that attained with thinner clothes.

The first Ching I made took about two hours, the last about one hour. It's really quite easy, and will save you a tidy chunk of cash.

CHAPTER 9

THE PRONE POSITION

The steadiest shooting position is prone, so let's start here.

ANALYSIS

In prone the body lies flat to almost flat on the ground. Both elbows are anchored on the ground, as is the shooter's chest. This forms a wide, heavy three-point triangular base, which simply cannot wobble much. The support arm bicep muscle is still doing the work of holding up the front end of the rifle, so here is where a shooting loop sling removes the last vestige of muscle stress from the equation. With a loop sling in prone, you can truly fall asleep in position without the rifle swaying off the target. The rifle butt must be in the "pocket." The support arm hand should, if possible, be run up against the sling swivel and wedged there in a relaxed state without any gripping tension.

Your breathing will tend to raise and lower your chest and shoulders, which will cause the rifle muzzle to pivot downwards as you inhale and vice-versa, so this is something to which you must pay attention. Your spine and the rifle are (as seen from the side) more or less in alignment with each other, and this position brings your face closest to the rear of your scope. This is where you will find out whether you have mounted your scope far enough forward to avoid getting whacked in recoil! It is also a posi-tion that will often require a bit of back-of-the-neck muscle tension to hold your head up so that your eye is behind the scope properly. If this becomes a prob-lem, you can either hook your shooting hand thumb over the stock comb and rest your cheek on your thumb instead of the stock, or acquire a pad for the stock comb to raise it up about half an inch or so. This can make a huge difference in comfort allowing a relaxed head position with proper cheek weld and eye position.

There are two accepted ways to as-sume the prone position. The first is the old-school military position, where the body is off at about a 30-degree angle to the line of the rifle barrel. The body is essentially flat on the ground, with the legs straight at the knee and spread apart by about two and a half to three feet be-tween the heels, toes pointing outwards.

The second is the more modern com-petition style, which aligns the body as closely as possible to the rifle, so as to keep recoil from making the shooter's body displace in a rotational fashion that pulls your sights sideways off target. The strong-side knee is drawn up high towards the hip, which raises the torso slightly off the ground, which minimizes the up-and-down motion imparted to the rifle by your breathing. I prefer this version myself, and so do target shooters who use it from 100 to 1000 yards. 'Nuff said, as far as I'm concerned.

In either position, keep the support elbow as directly under the gun as possible. This allows the sling to properly hold up the rifle, but may cause some distress to the muscles behind the support-side shoulder.

STEADY HOLD FACTORS FOR PRONE

To check all the steady hold factors in prone, start with your support side hand. It should be relaxed and the rifle lying from the center of the heel of the palm to the web between thumb and forefinger, along that curved "lifeline." Then move back to the support elbow, directly under the rifle. Then the sling loop should be high on your support upper arm. Then your spine should be about 10 to 25 degrees angled off to the support side of the rifle barrel. Your support side foot should be relaxed and drooping over to one side or the other. Your trigger side leg should be either straight and about 30-36 inches between your feet (old-fashioned prone) or have its knee drawn up as far as comfortable (new-fashioned prone). Your trigger side elbow should be planted on the ground but with less weight than the support side elbow. Your trigger hand grip should be firm but not tight, pulling the rifle into your shoulder, with your trigger finger not pulling wood on the stock. Your head should be extended all the way forward and dropped with relaxed neck onto the comb of the stock. Your cheek should form the correct stock weld or thumb weld to center your eye behind your sights. This latter is extremely important.

Be aware of where the sling loop is on your arm. As noted above, if it slides down your support side upper arm, it will have the same effect as lengthening the loop, allowing your support hand (and the rifle) to sag lower and reducing the overall steadiness of the position. Remember to start working on this position with the tightest, shortest loop length you can that allows the rifle butt to get into your shoulder pocket. If you need more loop length you can either adjust it the next notch longer, or try letting the loop slide down your arm slightly. But if you decide on a given loop length with the sling strap high on your support upper arm, don't let the strap slip down your upper arm or you will lose a great deal of support.

The sling loop length that works best for prone might be a bit too loose in the sitting position, so please take note of my comments in the sitting chapter as to how to best use one sling loop setting to work in both positions. If you are starting on prone and have not yet tried sitting, go ahead and find the best loop length for prone. Otherwise, you might simply want to use the sitting loop length and have the loop at a lower position on your support upper arm (closer to the elbow than the shoulder), which will allow for a shorter loop to still work.

ADJUSTING NATURAL POINT OF AIM

Get your horizontal NPA correct by rotating your whole body around your support elbow. Fine adjustments in horizontal NPA can be made by nudging your support elbow to the left or right. Adjust vertical NPA by moving the trigger-side elbow straight outwards to the side to lower your shoulder and raise the

The standing ready position.

Standing to prone: support arm goes into the sling as you drop.

On knees, placing buttstock on ground. Note support arm is in sling.

rifle muzzle, and vice versa. Generally a lower position will be a bit steadier than a higher one, but if you are using a shooting loop sling and have it adjusted to be a bit on the snug side, this will force a higher position that will still be extremely steady. This can be useful to get above the grass. If you want a lower position, lengthen your shooting loop (or let it slide down your support upper arm a bit) and your support hand will be able to sag down a bit lower.

STANDING TO PRONE

To get into prone from standing ready, turn slightly to the trigger hand side, and simply drop to your knees while holding the rifle vertically out in front of you, muzzle up. If you are using a Ching sling, loop up first as you start to drop. As your knees hit, lean forwards and

Lay forward onto strong hand and support elbow.

reach out with the butt of the rifle and plant it on the ground with the rifle still vertical. When the butt hits the ground, reach out with your trigger hand to support yourself as you go forwards into prone, bringing your support elbow to the ground ahead of you and brining the rifle down to horizontal with your support hand. From here, scoot your support elbow as far out in front of your body center as you can make it go.

With a sling, I find it useful to roll slightly to the support side, which allows me to get my support elbow out in front of my body centerline. I shoulder the rifle while still rolled onto my side, then I roll back flat on the ground and plant my trigger-side elbow. In this way I can get my support elbow in a position underneath where the rifle will be, and when I roll back onto my chest the rifle rotates up above my support elbow into the correct position. Remember to get your body angle to the target correct, as it helps put the rifle over the support elbow. That is why you make that slight turn to the trigger hand side when beginning to drop from standing to prone.

Prone position from the right. Support hand relaxed against sling swivel.

Scoot your support hand up to the front sling swivel and wedge it there in a relaxed condition with the swivel centered in the web between thumb and forefinger. If your arms are short or the sling attachment is very far forwards, this position may allow the rifle to droop too much; if so, you will have to grip the fore-end at some distance to the rear of that swivel. In prone is where the length of your sling loop really matters; if it is too short, you will not be able to get the butt in your shoulder, and if it is too long, the relaxation of your support arm against the sling will have the rifle droop too low. Fine tune the loop length so that the rifle is held horizontal by the sling and you can just get the butt in your shoulder without a big struggle.

The ideal position is one in which you can relax everything and the rifle is held right at the level you want it, and everything seems sort of wedged together under moderate pressure. You can maintain such a position for a long time, with such steadiness that the only visible motion of the rifle will be a slight up-and-down motion of the sight caused by the sling picking up the pulse from the artery in your upper arm. This motion is worth about half a minute of angle or so.

Note that when you inhale, your chest and shoulders will rise, and the rifle muzzle will dip, since it will pivot like a seesaw over your support hand. Varying the amount of air in your lungs can give you minute adjustments in aim elevation. Make sure you are consistent in how

Prone position from behind. Spine straight, support side leg straight in line with spine and foot relaxed, trigger side knee drawn up.

Prone position from the left. Sling well up on arm.

much air is in your lungs when you fire the shot. The simplest and most natural is to pause after normal exhalation and hold your breath there. Setting up your natural point of aim in elevation at this point in the breathing cycle gives you a naturally repeatable condition. And if the movement of the rifle sights up and down as you breathe is not in a vertical line but rather diagonal, make sure your support elbow is really under the rifle correctly.

If you are lying in a little depression or gully with your rifle poking out over the upper edge of it, the above position may have you pointing high due to the slope of the ground. A variation of prone that

Prone position from the front. Note the support elbow under the rifle.

Hawkins fist-rest-prone position: Your fist grabs the sling at the forward swivel and rests on the ground, the rifle rests on your fist.

works well here is the Hawkins prone or fist-rest. Rather than loop up in the sling, you simply grab the forward end of the rifle sling at the forward swivel, and with your fist resting on the ground, you let the rifle fore-end rest on your fist. This lowers your position quite a bit and supplies a fairly steady rest as well.

Prone will bring you in line with grass and bushes, so make sure your bullet has a clear path to the target, especially right in front of your muzzle. If you are lying on bare dirt or sand, and the wind is in your face, be prepared for a face-full of grit when you fire, since the muzzle blast of a centerfire rifle is quite powerful.

If using a hard rest (like a rock or log) from prone (or any position for that matter), never let any part of the rifle (especially the barrel!) touch it. Your support hand (or something soft like a glove, etc.)

only should contact the rest, and the rifle should only contact either this soft object or your hand. Otherwise the hard contact may change the bullet's impact through vibration bounce of the rifle away from a hard object.

THINGS TO AVOID

Avoid having your support elbow off to the outside of the rifle, as this will negate the value of the sling support and may allow the rifle to fall sideways towards the strong-hand side.

Avoid poor or improper cheek weld on the stock, as this will put your eye in a poorly-centered position behind the scope, possibly resulting in parallax error.

Avoid using muscle tension in your arms to either hold up the rifle or force it to point to your target if your NPA is off.

Avoid shooting into vegetation or a

hump in the ground ahead of you (remember that your scope will be about 1.5 inches above the bore line).

Avoid gripping the rifle fore-end with the support hand if possible, as varying grip pressure or tremors in the hand will cause rifle movement.

Avoid having the sling loop too loose (too long); the buttstock should be firmly wedged into your shoulder and your support arm should be able to stay dead limp.

Avoid letting the sling loop slide down your support upper arm as it will act as a too-loose loop.

Avoid letting comfort dictate the details of your position; maximum steadiness with maximum relaxation should be the guiding rule. A good prone position will NOT be very comfortable!

Prone seems to be the last position anyone thinks of when out in the woods, mainly because vegetation and uneven ground can obscure your view (and the bullet's flight). Even assuming a clear line to the target, for some reason lying on the ground just appears to put people off as undignified or something. However, watching people beat the snot out of the 12-inch ten ring on the 600 yard highpower rifle target using iron sights will make a believer out of you. That's roughly a two minute-of-angle circle. A good prone position will let you shoot two minutes or less and get your hits at ranges that will seem nothing short of fantastic – if you know what you are doing and do it right.

Learn early, practice often.

CHAPTER 10

THE SITTING POSITION

The most useful and versatile of all positions is, in my opinion, sitting. I consider it to offer the best combination of versatility, steadiness, and quickness of the lot. With mastery of this position along with using a shooting loop sling, you can accurately place shots out to 250 yards on a saucer-sized target. If you're a hunter, a quickly-assumed, rock-steady sitting position ought to be at the top of your list of preferred techniques. You will need to watch for any vegetation along your bullet flight path due to the position's closeness to the ground.

ANALYSIS

In this position, face your body enough to the trigger-hand side so that the rifle is directly over the support elbow – somewhere between 45 and 60 degrees to the side of your firing direction. The rump is firmly planted on the ground along with either the feet, the crossed legs, or the crossed ankles, and both elbows are solidly rested on the legs just ahead, or tucked inside the crook, of the knees. The weight of the arms and rifle is supported by the bones of the arms resting upon the bones of the legs. With a proper forward lean of the upper body, some of its weight is also supported by the arm and leg bones. Like prone, the only muscle tension really necessary should be in the support arm bicep. This should be replaced by the shooting loop sling, which, also taking on some of the weight of the forward-leaning upper body (as it pushes against the rifle buttplate), allows a very relaxed but extremely steady position.

Remember how I listed steady hold factors for prone in the preceding chapter, starting with the support hand and circling the body to end up at the trigger hand and head? Keep that theme in mind for all positions. The details from one to another may change, but if you check your steady hold factors using that circle in every position, you'll be unlikely to miss something important.

As far as the sitting position goes, the major difference from prone in those steady hold factors is what your legs are doing and where your elbows are planted. Support hand, elbow, sling position, trigger elbow, trigger hand, and head/cheek weld are the same. So, keep this "SHF" checking in mind as you read the following and start experimenting.

Of all the positions, sitting is the one that is most affected by a person's build. Whether you are long or short-limbed or long or short-bodied, or some mix, will dictate exactly which version of sitting you select and how you construct it. There are three varieties: open-leg, crossed-leg, and crossed-ankle. You will want to experiment with these positions, and pick the one that gives the best combination of steadiness, ease of acquisition, aiming ability, and comfort (with comfort being least important!). With all three there are two common characteristics you want to employ. The first is to have an aggressive forward lean with your upper body, bending from the hip/leg joints not waist so as to keep your back straight, so that relaxation makes your upper body settle forward onto your elbows and legs, without having to keep your stomach or back muscles tight to hold yourself in position. The second is to wedge your support hand against the front sling swivel so that the soft web of the hand between thumb and forefinger (not the base knuckle of the forefinger) is up against the swivel stud, with the hand relaxed and not gripping the fore-end. These two things are very important in eliminating sources of tremor in the position.

OPEN-LEG SITTING

The basic open-leg stance is easiest to assume and most versatile from a hunter's perspective, though crossed-leg and crossed-ankle positions, being steadier, are the norm in competition. Open-leg sitting allows for the rifle to be upright instead of tilted sideways as the cross-leg or cross-ankle positions often require, and allows radical change in NPA elevation by moving the feet towards or away from your body. Pivoting on your bottom applies horizontal NPA adjustments. Place your bottom well rearwards, so you get some degree of forward lean with your upper body. This is very important, so as to allow relaxation of the back and abdominal muscles, and to allow the

Open leg sitting from left.

Open leg sitting from right.

weight of your upper body and rifle to be supported by bone structure in your arms and legs. Spread your legs apart widely, but comfortably. Your legs should be oriented with the feet and knees pointing upwards or slightly inwards, rather than out to the sides. Make sure your heels are well planted, and let your feet just sort of hang loose. Any tension or squirming of your feet will cause your legs to move as a result. This is a bad thing, since you are going to be resting your elbows on your legs.

Avoid placing the points of your elbows on the points of your knees; they will wobble unsteadily. Instead, try to lean far enough forward so that your support arm elbow is just ahead of your knee, so the flat part of the back of your arm just above the elbow is resting on the flat part of your upper shin, just below the knee. If your support-side foot

is turned slightly inwards, it will make your upper shin a better support for your support elbow, which should rest slightly to the outside of the centerline of your leg. Again, have the back of your upper support arm resting just forward of the knee, and try to do the same with your trigger-side elbow. Or, tuck the point of your trigger-side elbow just below and inside the crook of the trigger-side knee; this will keep your elbow from being knocked off your knee by heavy recoil.

If you have a bit too much stomach, you may find it impossible to get your support elbow out in front of your knee. If this is the case, rest the base of your support forearm, just below the elbow, on the end of your thigh just above the knee. Be sure you have a good forward lean to the upper body when doing this, so that your upper body settles down onto your arm bones. You may find yourself applying tension to the groin muscles that bring your legs together. This is usually caused by having your knees beginning to sort of fall away from each other, to the outside. In this case your legs are rotated or twisted too much to the outside. Try to get a comfortable, solid position with your knees upright so that you don't use any outside hip or inner groin muscle tension to hold your legs in place. Try to let simple gravity do it for you.

Jam your support hand up against the sling swivel so that your hand contacts the swivel in the soft web between thumb and forefinger. Relax the hand; do not grip the fore-end as that will add some muscle jitter to your hold. If you are using a shooting loop sling it will provide all the tension necessary to keep support arm and rifle together. As in prone, if your arms are short or the front swivel is placed way out there, you may not be able to reach it, in which case you will be forced to grip the rifle fore-end with the support hand. If so, use the minimum grip force necessary and do not vary it.

CROSSED-LEG SITTING

Crossed-leg is having your legs tucked tightly under you. Have your trigger-side foot underneath your support-side knee so as to keep that

knee up high enough to help support the rifle in proper elevation alignment. Your body remains almost upright and you just sort of settle your elbows onto your legs. Again, the support elbow is best placed just ahead of your knee or shin. For people with long bodies or short arms, this is often an unsatisfactory position because it makes them have to slump down so far to get their elbows down to their legs that the gun tends to tilt over to the strong side and point to the ground not far in front of the shooter.

Open leg sitting from front.

Crossed leg sitting from right.

Crossed leg sitting from left.

Crossed leg sitting from front.

At this point you will have to slide your support hand back from the sling swivel and grip the fore-end closer to the receiver in order to raise the barrel back up to level. This can add some wobble to the position. People who are shorter or stockier than average seem to have the best luck with this position, but you never know until you try it. If you can pull it off it is very steady. Horizontal NPA adjustments are made by rotating on your butt. Elevation is controlled by how you have your elbows resting on your legs, or, you can raise your knees slightly by tightening the cross of your legs under each other (pushing your crossed legs more tightly together) and vice versa. Remember, you can also adjust your strong-side elbow to raise and lower your shoulder for elevation (raising and lowering the rifle butt with the shoulder, and causing the opposite movement of the muzzle as the rifle pivots over the support hand) as well as adjusting your support side elbow. Experiment!

CROSSED-ANKLE SITTING

Crossed-ankle opens this up a bit by pushing your ankles out in front of your body such that your knee joints are open at slightly more or less than 90 degrees and your ankles are now forward of your knees. Note that you want the support-side ankle to be on top of the trigger-side ankle, to gain the most elevation for the support-side knee. It requires an extremely aggressive forward lean of the upper body, which will be uncomfortable or even impossible for some people, but which greatly increases both the ability to relax the body and the steadiness of the position. You will probably find that this position will cause the gun to tilt over to the strong side to some degree.

Crossed ankle sitting from right. Note ankles well forward of knees.

This will cause your shots to go to that side and low compared to your aim unless you compensate by gripping the fore-end closer to the action, so as to raise the muzzle a bit which helps un-tilt the rifle. NPA adjustments are made the same way as in crossed-leg.

If you have a tendency to roll backwards when you relax and have to hold yourself upright with stomach muscle tension, push your butt further back. The idea is to have your upper body weight resting forward on your legs. However, many of you will find it at first difficult, if not impossible, to lean far enough forwards to develop a really stable position. The culprits are either too little flexibility in your lower back region, or just too much of you being compressed in front (or both!). Develop a safe and gentle stretching routine (you may want to check with your doctor for this) and lose those extra pounds! Actually, just continuous practicing of the sitting position is often enough to develop the required flexibility. Go gently and don't force anything – this writer knows all about torn lower back muscles, and wouldn't wish the same on anyone! This forward lean allows you to relax your upper body and let it slump forward, with the weight supported both by the bones of your arms and legs, and the sling strap freezing your support arm elbow. This gives you maximum stability with maximum relaxation. Remember that in this position your bones and the sling will give you nearly as much support as in the prone position, so always be alert to whether or not you are using muscle instead of the natural advantages of the position.

Watch how your front sight or crosshairs moves as you breathe. If it moves straight up and down, chances are your

Crossed ankle sitting from left.

Crossed ankle sitting from front.

position is good. If, on the other hand, it moves at a slant, you probably need to get that support elbow more directly under the rifle. Turning your body a little more towards the trigger hand side can help. Once you have settled on a position that works for you, get into the habit of always testing your NPA by assuming position, closing your eyes, relaxing without consciously trying to point the rifle any place in particular, then opening your eyes and seeing where the front sight or crosshairs put themselves. This is your natural point-of-aim. Adjust onto the target as necessary.

Be aware of where the sling loop is on your arm. As noted before, if it slides down your support side upper arm, it will have the the same effect as lengthening the loop, allowing your support hand (and the rifle) to sag lower and reducing the overall steadiness of the position. If you have worked on prone before trying sitting and have set your loop length for that position, you might need one notch less of length (tighter). Remember to start working on this position with the tightest, shortest loop length you can that allows the rifle butt to get into your shoulder pocket. If you need more loop length you can either adjust it the next notch longer, or try letting the loop slide down your arm slightly. But if you decide on a given loop length with the sling strap high on your support upper arm, don't let the strap slip down your upper arm or you will lose a great deal of support.

Generally, in the field you will be using one setting for your sling. Sometimes you will have time to change the loop length, but often not. Usually a good tight

loop for sitting will be a bit too short and tight to use for prone, unless you either let the loop slide down your support upper arm in prone (using the tighter sitting loop length) or use the longer prone setting for sitting, in which case you might not get enough support to maximize your steadiness. Your best bet will likely be to pick one setting and just modify how high or low the loop is on your upper arm to give the best tension in each position. This is important, so take some time to experiment between the two shooting positions with varying loop lengths and placements. It might pay large dividends in accuracy under field conditions.

STANDING TO SITTING

Once you find your best position, then you can practice getting into it quickly. Starting in standing ready with the rifle at port-arms, turn your body slightly more to the trigger hand side, cross your feet, and drop straight down into sitting. Sling up in the Ching as you go down, so that when your fanny hits the ground the sling is on your arm correctly, and your trigger hand is free to brace yourself as your fanny touches the ground. Assume what you believe to be your correct position; then, do the close-eyes-relax-open-eyes NPA test described previously. You will find that at first you'll need to do a lot of correcting. After a bit of regular practice, however, you'll be able to drop right into a very good sitting position and have your NPA coincide very closely to your target. Once this begins to happen, you will be able to hit that target at 200 yards with both a speed and a consistency that you would have thought impossible before! With careful position preparation, you

Standing to sitting: cross your feet & drop straight down while support arm slings up.

Butt hits ground, brace yourself with the trigger hand. Note support arm in sling and body faced about 45-55 degrees to strong side of target direction.

Into final position of choice.

More learning early, crossed-leg variation.

may be able to keep the wobble of your crosshairs within about a three minute-of-angle zone while being quite relaxed in your position, and be able to get your shot off within the inner two minutes of wobble. At 200 yards, that translates to a six-inch diameter wobble zone with a four-inch hit probability inside it.

In order to get the best out of this position, it will take some extra time perfecting the small details of exactly where your arms rest on your legs, how much forward lean you have, and how tight (very) the sling is. Don't stint on experimenting with these variables in large and small ways, even after you have decided upon which of the three versions to use. It is in perfecting these small details that the highest potential of this excellent position is realized. Keep at it and be patient!

WHAT TO AVOID

There are so many variables to the position that making a detailed list of errors is difficult.

Avoid improper placement (point on point) of the elbows on knees.

Avoid an upright or rearward-leaning position of the upper body (using back or stomach muscles).

Avoid facing the target too squarely with your chest, as this will force the support elbow to be off to the outside of the rifle.

Avoid unsteady placement of the legs, since everything else will be resting on them.

Avoid moving or tensing your feet or ankle joints.

Avoid canting of the rifle to the side.

Avoid any unnecessary muscle tension.

Avoid having the sling loop set too long (too loose) – it should be a tight loop with a strong "wedge fit" of the rifle in your shoulder.

Avoid letting the sling loop slide down your support upper arm unintentionally.

Avoid letting comfort dictate the details of your position; maximum steadiness with maximum relaxation should be the guiding rule.

A good sitting position will not necessarily be uncomfortable, but you won't know until you try!

If you are a hunter (especially in fairly open country), consider sitting your bread-and-butter position. While it has some drawbacks in brushy terrain or when facing uphill, it will cover more types of situations with more quickness, steadiness, and range than just about every other position. With a well-developed and well-practiced position, and a tight Ching sling loop, you should be able to get into position from standing in five to seven seconds (if you are limber), and be steady enough to hit a target the size of a saucer at 250 yards quite consistently.

CHAPTER 11

SQUATTING AND KNEELING POSITIONS

The squatting and kneeling positions are quite quick and useful out to 100-150 yards. They are slower to acquire, but more steady, than the standing position, and faster to acquire than, but not as steady as, sitting. You will need to note if there are intervening obstacles to vision or bullet flight at this position elevation level. If you have a clear sight line to the target midway to the ground, and the target is beyond your confident offhand range but vegetation or rocks preclude sitting or prone, and time may be of the essence, these positions are a good choice. They are quick to acquire and exit, especially when on the move before and after the shot, and so are especially useful to the soldier. Let's look at the squat first.

SQUATTING: ANALYSIS

Your body is supported on its feet as in standing, yet is folded up and compressed as much as possible. This eliminates virtually all points of swaying and motion above the ankle joints. The elbows are partially but adequately supported by the inside of the knees. The sight line is low, so watch out for vegetation. The wider your feet are planted, the more stable the stance. Due to the small base of support, heavy recoil may knock you right over. Again, the support arm bicep is working, so the shooting loop sling is indicated.

Simply squat down as deeply as you can, feet flat on the ground, and tuck your elbows inside your knees. Have your chest facing about as far off the line of fire as in standing (80-85 degrees to the trigger hand side).

Your support elbow should be as directly under the rifle as possible. Horizontal NPA corrections are made by rotating your body with your feet. Elevation changes are limited by how much you can squirm your elbows around between your knees. There may be a tendency to rock or bounce a bit immediately on assuming this position, so wait a few seconds to settle down if necessary. Keep your feet as far apart as comfortably possible to make your support base as wide as possible, since it will help reduce body sway and also help prevent a heavy-recoiling gun from knocking

Squatting from front.

Squatting from right. Note elbows tucked inside knees.

Squatting from left.

you off balance. Steady hold factors are similar: support hand relaxed and open, sling high on your support arm, elbows tucked between knees, feet as wide apart as practical, firm grip with right hand pulling rifle into shoulder, trigger finger not pulling wood, your head as forward as possible and laying relaxed on the stock with a good cheek weld. Don't forget to loop up in your Ching sling on the way down!

Be aware of where the sling loop is on your arm. As noted above, if it slides down your support side upper arm, it will have the same effect as lengthening the loop, allowing your support hand (and the rifle) to sag lower and reducing the overall steadiness of the position. You should use whatever sling loop length you have decided upon when working with the sitting position. This length should work here, but if you need to have slightly more or less loop length, try letting the loop slide up or down your arm slightly. But if you decide on a given loop length with the sling strap high on your support upper arm, don't let the strap slip down your upper arm or you will lose a great deal of support.

SQUATTING: WHAT TO AVOID

Avoid crashing down into the position abruptly, as you may lose your balance when you hit bottom, and you will certainly be bobbing around for a bit even if you don't.

Avoid keeping your feet too close together, or recoil will roll you right over.

Avoid shooting before your body has settled down into the position.

Avoid letting the sling loop slide down your support upper arm.

More learning early.

KNEELING: ANALYSIS

The body is supported by the support-side foot, the strong-side knee, and the strong-side toes, with the rump sitting upon the strong-side heel. Both legs are bent at tighter than 90 degrees at the knee joint, with the strong-side leg folded back on itself and the support-side leg nearly so (having a more open support-side leg requires tension in the hamstring muscle on the back of the thigh, which can induce tremors to the position). Try to keep your support-side leg angled so that its foot is not to the rear of its knee. The foot should be directly under or ahead of the knee. Otherwise, your balance will be poor, and falling on your face is a possibility. This forms a fairly steady three-point triangular base on the ground.

The support-side elbow is rested just ahead of the support-side knee. However, the strong-side elbow is dangling in the air, which greatly reduces horizontal steadiness of the upper body. The support arm bicep is working, so use the loop sling to eliminate this. Except for leg positioning and elbow placement, steady hold factors are similar to squatting.

Kneeling provides great steadiness in the vertical plane (when used with a loop sling!), but allows enough sideways swaying to make the position problematic beyond a fairly short range. This can be improved with certain modifications. Disregard any photographs you may have seen of kneeling shooters with their support elbow dangling in the air. That elbow belongs solidly rested on the support side knee – actually, just ahead of it. Point-to-point contact of elbow on knee tends to wobble. Rest the back of your upper arm just above the elbow on the front of your knee, just below the bend. The strong-side knee is on the ground.

The conventional position has the strong-side foot set vertical on the toes, with the rump sitting on the heel. A variation is to turn the strong-side foot sideways so it is flat on the ground, with the rump sitting on the ankle. When using this variant, have your support-side foot placed several inches further ahead of the knee, to allow a good forward lean into the position. This variant takes about a second longer to get into, but gets you a bit lower down to the ground. Horizontal NPA corrections are made by turning the entire body from the ground up, pivoting on the forward foot (though pivoting on the trigger side knee/foot also works). Elevation changes are somewhat limited, requiring sliding the support elbow up or down the front of the support side knee, moving the support-side foot forward or rearward to lower or raise the knee, and perhaps a bit of upper-body slumping to lower the rifle-bearing shoulder in order to pivot the muzzle upwards a bit.

The sideways swaying can be reduced if you lean the outside of your support forearm against some vertical surface such as a tree. This greatly improves the position. With a horizontal rest available at the right height, you can use the supported reverse-kneeling position. In this, the support-side knee is on the ground, and the back of the support hand is lying on the rest. The trigger-side knee is up, and the trigger-side elbow is resting on it. The horizontal rest provides both vertical and horizontal support to the hand, and the trigger-side high knee supporting the trigger-side elbow improves the horizontal stability of the body.

Kneeling from front. Note the support elbow under the rifle and the trigger elbow is high.

Kneeling from right. Note high trigger-side elbow.

Kneeling from left. Note the support elbow ahead of the knee.

Reverse supported kneeling. Note the support hand on tree branch stub and reversed knee positions.

The height of the rest is critical here. If it is too high you will not be able to settle down in the position enough to get your trigger-side elbow down on your knee. In this position, keep your trigger-side foot spread as far out to the trigger side as is comfortably possible. This will broaden your body's base of support, thus reducing the side-to-side swaying motion of your upper body.

The sling comments from squatting apply here equally. To get into position, simply take one step forward with the support side foot and then drop straight down until your trigger-side knee is on the ground.

KNEELING: WHAT TO AVOID

Avoid point-on-point contact of the support elbow and knee.

Avoid snatching at the trigger if you find yourself swaying a bit too much from side to side (assume a steadier position of that is the case).

Avoid letting the sling loop slide down your support upper arm.

CHAPTER 12

THE STANDING POSITION

The standing position, being the least steady, is what you use when no steadier one is possible, due to time constraints, intervening vegetation, etc. There are three general variants of this stance: the rearward-leaning, bone-supported stance of the target shooter; the forward-leaning stance similar to a shotgun trapshooter's stance; and one that splits the difference by being normally erect. Terminology of whether one is in the "standing" position versus the "offhand" position can vary by user, so I will go by the terminology just described.

ANALYSIS

This stance is anchored on the ground by two feet spaced about shoulder width or slightly more apart. Above that we have flexible ankle joints, followed by flexible knee joints, followed by flexible hip joints, and a flexible spine. In two out of the three position variants, the rifle is held up by the support arm without having any solid rest, so a shooting loop sling, while helping eliminate support arm bicep stress, is of limited value – the support arm shoulder muscle (the deltoid) is still holding up both arm and rifle. Go ahead and use the hasty sling anyway, as it will help dampen tremors in the support arm. NRA bullseye rules don't apply in the field! The third variant is the target shooter stance, where the support arm is folded double and pulled back against the side of the body. In this position the rifle weight is supported by the vertical upper and lower arm bones, which in turn are supported by the rib cage. Meanwhile, everything else below that is still swaying in the breeze. The obvious challenge here is how to minimize all that.

The target shooter's stance brings the upper body back away from the target, so that the support upper arm can fold tightly back against the ribcage. The support forearm is vertical. The hand is open, palm horizontal and facing up, fingers either pointed towards the target or to the support side, with the rifle simply lying on it at about the magazine floorplate position, without being gripped by the fingers. It is wise to have the thumb on one side of the rifle and the other four fingers on the other side, since this allows a quick grasp to be made if necessary, if the rifle starts to fall off the palm or when rapidly working the bolt.

Alternatively, the fingers can be extended so that the tip of the thumb is under the trigger guard, and the other fingertips are supporting the rifle under the magazine floorplate. I prefer not to use the fingertip support because of the potential for wiggle and muscle fatigue in both the fingers and the wrist joint. If the rifle is lying flat on your horizontal palm, there is neither finger action (as long as you keep them relaxed) nor wrist action, since the weight of the rifle will stabilize the relaxed wrist at about its furthest range of motion (the principle of shooting against your ligaments). The weight of the rifle is transmitted through the support arm bones directly to the torso; there is no arm or shoulder muscle involved. Because of this the position does not induce much muscle fatigue in the support arm over a long period of time.

The buttstock will have to be placed quite a bit higher on your shoulder than usual to bring the stock comb up to your cheek properly. Keep the strong-side elbow high (arm horizontal) to accentuate the shoulder "pocket" for the buttstock. The feet should be pointed more towards the strong side than towards the target. The knees may be locked, or just short of locked. I find that locked knees tend to accentuate swaying of my body from the ankle joints while disallowing slight flexing of the knee joints to counter the

ankle motion. You will have to experiment. Steadiness comes from having the legs and hips as stable as possible, with the upper body sort of slumped down in a relaxed position, so it reaches the natural limits of its motion and does not have the tendency to move about any further. Some muscle tension is necessary throughout the body to minimize swaying, and this is something that requires experimentation. NPA adjustments for elevation are made by moving the rear foot towards the target (lowering your muzzle) or away from the target (raising your muzzle). Horizontal NPA adjustments are made by moving the rear foot to the right or left of the line of fire.

With development and practice, this can be a quite steady position. It is a bit slower to assume than the other positions, and is designed for shooting one shot at a time, at a sedate pace. This is the position that highpower bullseye shooters use to hit the seven-inch ten ring at 200 yards. I do not use this position in the field, but one of my fellow highpower shooters once used it to take a buck at about 200 yards. A very explicit description of how to build this position can be found in G. David Tubb's book "Highpower Rifle." Mr. Tubb, eleven-time national highpower bullseye champion, uses this to aim for the three-inch diameter X-ring at 200 yards.

The forward-leaning "trapshooter" stance is what I favor, probably because I used to do a lot of shotgunning. Mount the rifle correctly as described earlier. Lean your body weight well forward. You will probably want to take a slight step forwards with the support side leg when assuming this position from ready. The

Standing trapshooter from right. Note slight forward lean, stock brought up to erect head, and high trigger-side elbow.

lead leg should be bent at the knee. Face your chest about 80 degrees off the line of fire, your front foot pointed towards the target. Keep your support elbow directly under the gun. The support hand should firmly grip the rifle at the fore-end. Keep the strong-side elbow high to form the "pocket."

This is a very fast position to assume, but relies entirely on muscle to hold, so it is best for a fairly quick shot. The forward weight bias allows for rapid recovery from recoil, and the firm grip of the support hand allows for control of the rifle when rapidly working the action with the strong hand. This is an excellent position from which to take the snap shot, described below. The use of NPA in this position is somewhat limited, since the time factor involved when using this position will almost certainly be very short, and the ability to relax into your position is slight. The best approach to getting on your target at the instant of mounting will simply be muscle memory from a large amount of practice.

The normally-erect position places the body just so. The spine is straight. The support arm is well bent, with the hand cradling, but not gripping, the rifle under the magazine, and the elbow directly under the rifle. The strong-side elbow is high to form the "pocket." Body weight is centered between the feet, which are slightly more than shoulder width apart. This is perhaps a better position than the "trapshooter" if you may be taking more time to aim, since its lack of forward lean reduces muscle tension.

If you are forced to take a long shot from standing due to terrain considerations, choose the target shooter stance.

Of the other two positions, I tend to favor the trapshooter stance primarily for speed and recoil resistance, as well as habit and familiarity.

Experiment with the two and draw your own conclusions. In either of these two positions, try to keep your muscle tension in the support arm and hand at an absolute minimum. Too much there will cause the rifle to twitch and jerk almost uncontrollably. Relaxing the rest of your body, especially your abdominal muscles, as much as possible will also help.

Practice standing intensely and often, in dry fire. Take care to start the motion correctly with a proper gun mount. If your mount is bad, it will ruin the whole motion.

Since the standing positions rely so much on sheer muscle, and since no one can hold perfectly steady, there is quite a challenge to controlling the motion of the gun. With a great deal of practice, one's muscles will become conditioned to hold ever more steady, but the problem remains. One means to this end that has been developed by target shooters is to actually move the rifle in a slow, controlled motion across the target and fire at the correct instant when the aim is just right. There is something about guiding the rifle movement in one direction that, for some reason, seems to negate a lot of the random, multi-directional twitches you see when trying to hold it still.

In his book, G. David Tubb describes coming into the target from the side in a horizontal motion. I prefer a vertical motion, preferably straight downwards. This allows the rifle to move in the direction that the prevailing force against it (gravity) wants to make it go, and by letting

Standing erect from right. Note erect head, and high trigger-side elbow.

Standing target from right. Note erect head, high trigger-side elbow, rearward lean, and folded support arm resting against body with near-vertical arm bone positions.

Standing target from front. Note reversed support hand position and curved, slumping spine.

my muscles "go with the flow" it seems to reduce a lot of the work my muscles would otherwise be doing. The result is that if my horizontal NPA is lined up with the target, the rifle moves straight downwards smoothly and without much, if any, sideways movement, and hardly any sudden twitches or jerks. This creates a slow, smooth, predictable motion that allows fairly precise timing of the trigger press (a very short compressed surprise break).

Remember that by the time all your physiological processes of seeing, deciding, and moving your trigger finger are completed, and all the mechanical processes of the rifle's trigger mechanism, firing pin, gunpowder combustion, and bullet motion through the barrel are completed, the barrel will have moved past your "shoot now" decision point, and your bullet will hit past your aimpoint in the direction the rifle was moving. Shoot on the way in to your desired impact point, just before your sight crosses it, not directly at it. If shooting on the move is too difficult for you, practice the moving-in of the rifle and then pause at the correct place for the shortest time possible for you to get off the shot.

In live fire, note the maximum distance at which you can keep all of your shots inside the eight-inch black of that smallbore target. This is your maximum big-game range for standing. You may find it distressingly short. No matter; keep practicing. Great improvements can be made with lots of dry fire practice. Remember, never shoot from this position unless all others are impossible, and never beyond your maximum range.

USING A REST IN STANDING

When in the field, lean against a tree or rock if possible. If placing the rifle to the right of a vertical object, place the support hand flat against the near side of the support object with fingers up, and extend the thumb sideways toward the rifle and lay the rifle on top of the thumb without the rifle touching the object. If you are shooting past the left side of a vertical object, place the palm and lower three fingers on the object with the fingers pointing downrange and the thumb pointing up. Extend the forefinger sideways, lay the fore-end of the rifle in the crook of the thumb and forefinger without it touching the support object, and grasp the fore-end with these two fingers.

Important: Do not let the rifle fore-end or barrel touch the object! These instructions are for right-handers; southpaws reverse as necessary. Take careful note of the illustrations. When using these techniques, remember that you will only be as steady as your body. If you are swaying about, your support hand will act as a fulcrum as the rifle seesaws back and forth. Set your feet wide apart and bend your knees slightly to lower your center of gravity and steady yourself. Lean your body weight into the support hand that is rested against the object, if possible.

THE SNAPSHOT

A special-purpose variation of standing is the snapshot. From standing ready (rifle at port-arms, rifle butt at hip, muzzle in line between eye and target), try for a fast mount with an instant line-up with the target. The forward lean stance works well for this. At 25 yards, use a target diameter of about four inches. At 50 yards,

Standing rest to right of vertical object. Rifle rests on thumb of support hand without touching object.

Standing rest to right of vertical object, opposite side view.

Standing rest to left of vertical object. Rifle rests on web between forefinger base knuckle and thumb of support hand without touching object.

Standing rest to left of vertical object, opposite side view.

The standing ready position.

use the eight-inch smallbore target black. Time limit is 1.5 seconds! Consider this an advanced drill, not to be attempted until you are comfortable with slow-fire standing. The key to making the time limit is a perfect gun mount that presents the eye with a view of your target already centered by the crosshairs. This, as you can imagine, takes a lot of practice. Work towards a perfect mount, slowly and consistently, until you can get that instant full field of view through the scope with your crosshairs on or very close to the target every time. Does having a correct natural point of aim in your stance help here? You bet! Get this down slow and smooth at first, then go for speed.

THINGS TO AVOID

This position is so unsteady that there is no end of challenge in it. The worst situation most people find themselves in is to be swaying all over the place, often while breathing heavily from either buck fever, climbing up the hill, or a sudden sprint to get to a place from which to see or shoot. Wild gyrations of the rifle tend to make people try to jerk the trigger whenever the rifle gets even vaguely near the aiming point. Avoid this by being in control of your breathing and your exertion levels, and work to make your position settle down. If you can't make the shot, well, you can't make the shot. Don't just fling lead out there carelessly.

Instant mount for the snapshot.

Avoid hunching your head down to the rifle stock. Rather, keep your head erect and bring the rifle stock up to your face. The top of the butt should end up a little above your shoulder.

Another thing to avoid is avoidance of practice! Standing-up shooting takes a large amount of consistent practice; don't stint on it. Remember, dry fire can be done in the home (carefully!) and doesn't cost anything but a little bit of time.

Bring the stock up to your face, so the butt rises above your shoulder.

CHAPTER 13

USING A REST

Okay, now we finally get to everybody's favorite way of shooting. The use of a rest is something we'd always like to take advantage of, whenever possible. There are two basic types: the ones we bring with us into the field (a sandbag, a bipod, shooting sticks, or even some part of our gear like a backpack) and ones that we find available as expedients (a log, a rock, a hump in the earth). Even in offhand, as detailed in the previous chapter, we can take advantage of what nature offers us.

There are a few rules that we need to observe while using any kind of rest. First, make sure that the barrel never touches any part of the rest! The resultant rebound of the barrel off any object while in firing vibration mode will throw your shot off zero. Second, make sure that even the fore-end is not sitting on something hard without some form of padding. If you are using a rock or a log, place your hand, or a glove, or a hat, or something similarly soft between the fore-end and the rest to reduce vibration rebound.

Third, you still have to apply some of the rules of position shooting as described earlier to steady your body. Just because the fore-end of the rifle is rested won't help you hold the crosshairs on your desired aim-point if your body is swaying in the wind like a stalk of grass. Fourth, if your rest position is low to the ground, make sure that you aren't shooting through vegetation. Remember that your scope is going to be looking about one and a half inches higher than your bore line, so double check where your barrel is looking. Hitting the grass three feet in front of your muzzle is going to mess up your shot.

And remember that nothing says you can't use the loop sling in conjunction with a rest (no, it's really not cheating!). This is especially useful to remember if your rifle has a change of zero between using the sling in position versus shooting off a benchrest. If this is the case, think about zeroing your rifle from position with the sling and using it even when you use a rest.

Remember that the principles of position shooting were formulated to steady the rifle by steadying the entire body. Just because you have a rest for the fore-end of the rifle, doesn't mean you can forget about steadying your body. For example, I recently saw a picture in a gun magazine of a man shooting a rifle from sitting using shooting sticks held in his support-side hand. I can't remember if his support-side elbow was rested on his support-side knee, but I definitely remember that his trigger-side elbow was dangling in the air. This represents failure to steady the upper body (with its buttstock-to-shoulder index) to the greatest degree possible. Even with sticks, bipod or another rest, get your body as steady as you can. Otherwise your swaying body will simply cause the rifle to tilt and seesaw over the rest. Use the principles of good position to make the entire shooting platform (rifle and shooter) steady even when the fore-end is artificially supported. It will allow you to use the rest to its fullest potential.

BIPODS

Let's look at the man-made rest aids first. Bipods are pretty popular, but have some limitations. First, you have to unfold them and get the leg length set right. This takes more time than just dropping into position while looping up in a Ching. In side-sloping terrain this may take considerably more time. Remember that the rifle must not be canted to one side. Bipods that have a side-to-side swivel ability will allow greater flexibility in aligning your position with the target, but may reduce steadiness somewhat as a consequence. Ditto for those types that allow cant flexibility. In any case, you want to construct a very steady body position using the techniques described previously. Such details as resting your strong-side elbow on your strong-side knee to stabilize the strong-side shoulder

in the sitting position are often forgotten by bipod users (just look at any shooting magazine for photographic evidence).

It is almost as though people think that the bipod works such steadying magic that nothing else matters. Whatever position you are in, make that position as perfect as possible to attain full body stability. And don't forget to check your natural point of aim! If you insist on using a bipod instead of a shooting loop sling, you can still have a loop sling on your rifle and use it together with the bipod. In sitting it will allow you to create the "lean your body into the sling" forward-leaning-rest position that can stabilize your body in a way that the bipod cannot provide. Also, leaning into the bipod used alone, so that the rifle is pressed forward against its legs, can help keep the bipod feet from jerking back across the ground due to recoil.

I suppose I'm probably just an aesthetic snob, but I like neither the weight nor the looks of a bipod on a deer/elk rifle. If you are a coyote caller, a bipod makes great sense in that it frees up the support hand to hold the call while the strong hand stays in firing position. On a specialized long-range rifle like a varmint rig, a target rig, or a sniper rifle, they certainly have their place (I still think they're ugly though). Even on such rifles, having a military M1907-type or Ching sling on them is a good idea, since it makes the shooting loop available if desired. On a deer/elk rifle, a bipod suggests to me that, um, the owner doesn't know how to shoot. Ahem. My own experience with them is admittedly limited to one session on prairie dogs with a heavy varmint rifle, so I may be missing something, but to me they

Prone with bipod. Use the normal prone position without change, or brace your support hand under your trigger fist or the buttstock.

Sitting with bipod. Note both elbows resting on knees. Use normal sitting position, or brace your support hand under your trigger fist or the buttstock.

are clumsy, ugly, heavy, and slow for all but specialized long-range use. I already know what I can do with a Ching sling, I can do it faster than everybody I've ever seen deploying and adjusting a bipod, and I'll put my practical accuracy on a deer-sized target up against theirs any day. If, on the other hand, your body simply won't allow itself to go into a standard target-shooting-with-a-loop-sling position (my friend with six fused spinal vertebrae comes to mind) a bipod or set of sticks is heaven-sent.

SHOOTING STICKS

Shooting sticks are essentially a bipod you carry separate from the rifle. Depending on the design, you may or may not have to hold them in place with the support hand (most don't require holding). Since the rifle is not attached, you can have the sticks canted on a side-slope and just lay the rifle in the crook in a normal upright fashion. Height is quickly adjustable by how wide you open the sticks. However, if you are shifting your aim sideways enough to have to move the sticks over, you have to do so with your hand picking them up and moving them over since they are separate from the rifle.

Sticks have to be accessed from wherever you hid them before you can deploy them, so they might be a bit slower than a bipod. Again, they are not as fast as slinging up while dropping into position. Sticks don't clutter up your rifle like a bipod, and if I encounter you in the woods with your sticks hidden away I won't automatically consider you a duffer. Ahem.

When using a rest under the fore-end of your rifle, your support hand will now be free of the duty of holding onto the fore-end. You can continue to do so in the normal way, or you can brace your support hand under your trigger hand, or under the buttstock at your shoulder. Go ahead and experiment, but whatever you try, make sure you are not introducing more tremors. If your body position is good according to the rules for that position, you technically shouldn't need any extra help from your support hand, but you have to do something with it. A predator hunter can use that hand to blow a mouth call.

OTHERS

Having a sandbag in your pack may help if you anticipate taking a long prone shot in open country, but try filling it with something lighter than sand (like plastic beads) unless you're training for a triathlon.

Equipment-expedient rests will be familiar to readers of those late, lamented gentlemen Jack O'Connor and Elmer Keith. The former liked to use his daypack or binocular case, and the latter was known to use his famous big cowboy hat. The deal here is that height issues can be a problem; too much or too little to properly align with your intended target.

In prone you can cheat your strong-side elbow in or out to raise or lower your shoulder, but when using this sort of rest over a rock or log in sitting or kneeling, your elevation change options are few. Again, make sure that if your rest object is hard, you get something soft between it and the rifle fore-end.

FIELD-EXPEDIENT

Field-expedient rests are whatever Mother Earth offers: fallen trees, rock

Prone over day pack with sling. Note the support hand between rifle and rest.

outcrops, tree limbs of the right height, or just a well-placed bump in the ground. Let us assume for the moment that if you need a rest, the shot will probably be long and the animal may be unaware of your presence. This may give you a few extra seconds to sort things out (if the wind doesn't switch and send it your scent). Use those extra seconds to be sure that your lines of sight and bullet flight to the target are clear of the weeds. Once these criteria are met, pick the rest position that best allows you to use the principles of position to steady your body. You may have multiple fallen trees or rock outcrops, for example; find the one that offers the best ability to put your body in a comfortable and steady position.

As stated before, having something solid on which to rest your rifle is only of limited help if your body is wobbling about like a drunken sailor who hasn't yet gotten his land legs. And make sure to place soft padding between the rest object and the rifle fore-end.

Whenever you have a rest available take advantage of it, but give some serious thought to its best use. Consider that a rest should not be thought of as an alternative to skilled position shooting, but rather as a complement to it. It is nice to not have to be dependent upon rests to be able to hit your target.

CHAPTER 14

TERMINAL BALLISTICS

"Terminal ballistics" is a fancy term for what a bullet does when it hits an object. From a hunting standpoint, this is very important, as it can make the difference between an impact that merely wounds an animal, or one that delivers a quickly fatal injury. Bullets are designed to do different things for different purposes, so it is up to us to recognize the differences and choose wisely.

Basically, for non-dangerous medium to big game purposes, we need a bullet that will both expand to some extent and penetrate through the animal's body deeply enough to inflict fatal damage to the heart/lung area. This is complicated by such factors as variations in bullet strength and bullet impact velocity, size and composition of the game animal, internal body structures encountered by the bullet, and angle of impact on the animal body.

Excessive expansion from weak bullet construction or excessive impact velocity can lead to inadequate penetration or even bullet fragmentation. Inadequate expansion from low impact velocity or overly strong bullet construction usually yields great penetration but small temporary and permanent wound channels. The causes of these two problems can be poor choice or use of bullet by the hunter, so let's take a look at it.

Most bullets are a compromise. A typical .30 caliber 150 grain bullet can be fired by a .300 Savage at 2600 feet per second or by a .300 Weatherby Magnum at 3300 feet per second. The former hitting a deer at 300 yards will produce a different stress on the bullet than the latter hitting a deer at 50 yards. Usually, a manufacturer of ammunition will make slightly different variants of the same bullet to overcome this, and will put the right version in the appropriate cartridge. But, if you are reloading your own ammunition, make sure you know what you are grabbing off the shelf.

Further, some bullets are specially designed for a certain purpose. For example, a bullet designed for varmint hunting is rather fragile and will fly to pieces quickly. This makes for a very well-splattered prairie dog or woodchuck, but can cause a painful but shallow surface wound on a deer's shoulder muscle. Such bullets usually cannot make it through a deer leg or shoulder bone into the chest cavity. If you can slip one between the ribs on a broadside shot it will often flatten an animal right there, but conversely if it hits a rib it might not even make it through.

In the early and middle years of the 20th century, there were quite a few problems caused by the introduction of higher and higher velocity cartridges making existing bullets blow up on impact. By now this is no longer a real problem; however we still need to make appropriate choices. But based on what? And we have a lot of choices: partition bullets, X-bullets, bonded bullets, locked-core bullets, plastic tips, varmint vaporizers, all from various makers. What should we choose, and what should we avoid?

From the perspective of hunting critters from antelope to big bears, let's first look at what to avoid. Varmint type bullets are out, due to their disintegrating nature. They will not penetrate a large animal deeply enough to reach the vitals. At the other end of the spectrum, a full metal jacket military spitzer "ball" type or roundnose "solid" bullet will usually drill a small hole with little damage (though a ball spitzer will often turn over rear-end first inside a body, making a mess while transiting sideways).

The only real application for a solid is in Africa on very big critters who don't take kindly to being shot, or perhaps hunting the largest bears with a large-caliber rifle. This also holds true for .22 rimfire bullets. A solid .22 will kill, but often the animal runs far enough to get away before it dies. Target type bullets, while being highly accurate and having a high ballistic coefficient, often are not designed to expand like a hunting bullet.

You have to follow the manufacturer's recommendation with these bullets. So, we want to avoid these types of bullets for typical, non-dangerous medium to big game.

What we really need first is enough straight-line penetration to reach the vitals from even a raking angle shot. The bullet must reach the heart/lung area on a body shot to be effective. In order to do this, the bullet might have to get through thick layers of wet fur, fat, and muscle, smash through bone, and on big animals penetrate as much as two feet or more of critter without going to pieces or being deflected from its original line of travel. If the bullet exits, so much the better. Some hold that this is a waste of bullet energy, but I believe otherwise, and will explain why further along.

Secondly, we would like some expansion of the bullet to create a larger wound channel. A body-shot animal dies from bleeding out internally (unless the spine is hit far enough forward to stop the heart), so the more damage we can do the quicker the death. Here is where we generally encounter the problem: too much expansion usually reduces penetration, and too weak a bullet may fly to pieces before it gets where we need it to go.

For a small animal like an antelope or the smaller deer, rapid expansion and shallower penetration is usually okay. For an elk or moose, it may result in a running wounded animal. On a grizzly bear, it can get you eaten.

Conversely, zero expansion usually has a similar effect, so a non-expanding solid bullet is a bad idea except for really huge, big-boned critters like elephant and African buffalo that require the penetration only a solid can give. One exception to this is the large-caliber flat-nose heavy lead bullet used in cartridges like the .45-70 and big-bore revolver magnum cartridges. These rounds make a fairly large hole to start with, impart a lot of battering energy with their flat noses, and with their great weight and front-to-rear near equal balance (which prevents the bullet from doing a 180 degree end-for-end flip) will make a very, very, long, straight, bone-smashing wound channel, usually with an exit, that really puts a stomping on the recipient.

So, we have to match the balance of expansion and penetration to the size of the animal we are after. Up to the size of whitetail deer, almost any good modern bullet will do. On larger animals, while rapid expansion bullets can make spectacular kills, it is best to err on the side of controlled expansion, greater bullet strength and retained weight, and deeper penetration. This is especially true with animals that can bite you. A structural-breakdown shot, such as through both front shoulder joints or a hip joint, may be necessary to prevent a justifiably angry wounded grizzly from discovering that you really do "taste just like chicken!"

Two other factors besides bullet construction are worthy of our consideration if we are to completely understand this topic. One is that every rifle barrel has a given rifling twist rate, which is calculated to properly stabilize a bullet within a given range of overall length. The longer the bullet, the faster the twist rate needs to be to achieve stability. The other factor is that increasing a bullet's weight means increasing its length, and sometimes, increasing a bullet's ballistic coefficient

also means increasing its length while not changing its weight (the Berger Very Low Drag match bullet is an example of this). Exceptions are bullets made of materials heavier than lead, which allow greater than usual weight while maintaining length within the normal range of lead bullets.

A heavier bullet has more mass and momentum, and while it will start off slower than a lighter bullet, it will retain its velocity better (with equal shapes) than the lighter bullet which will eventually slow down to below the velocity of the heavier bullet at longer ranges. The heavier bullet will generally deliver deeper penetration on game. The ratio of a bullet's mass to its cross-sectional area is called sectional density (S.D.). The heavier the bullet in a specific caliber, the higher the S.D. These factors are important as the choice of bullet weight and length requires knowing if a particular bullet is too long for our rifle's twist rate, which could be the case with certain specialty heavy bullets (like the Berger VLD), or knowing whether or not we have enough bullet weight for the animal we are hunting. Generally the bigger the animal you are after, the heavier you want your bullet to be in order to gain deep penetration and to smash through heavy bones without having the bullet destroy itself in the process.

So where does that point us in the bewildering array of modern bullets? Let's look at all the different construction types first.

The basic type is cup-and-core: a lead slug squeezed into a tube (or jacket) of thin sheet copper alloy that is closed at one end. A military full metal jacket ball bullet has the closed end of the copper jacket at its point and the open end at its base. A hunting bullet is the reverse, with some exposed lead (a "soft point"), or plastic (Nosler'sBalllistic Tip), or a small hollow point at the front end, and a fully enclosed base. Once manufacturers figured out the right combination of jacket thickness, jacket hardness, and lead softness/hardness for a given range of impact velocities, these have worked quite well. Their primary weakness is a tendency of the lead core to slide out of the jacket, which leads to either fragmentation of the core or changing bullet paths, and usually less penetration.

Next come the many enhancements to the cup-and-core. The purpose of these changes is to allow good bullet performance over a wider range of impact velocities, preventing bullet blow-up at high velocities while still allowing good expansion at low velocities. They strengthen the bullet, often increasing overall weight retention after expansion and deepening penetration. Let's start with the copper jacket.

Various manufacturers have tried varying the thickness of the copper jacket, making it thinner at the point to allow quick expansion while making it thick towards the base to resist too much expansion. Nosler and Swift have used this. Often the forward part of the jacket is scored with cuts to promote a banana-peel effect during expansion. Another jacket modification is the creation of a ridge or ring on the inside of the jacket to grab hold of the core and prevent core-jacket separation. The Remington Core-Lokt and Hornady Interlock are prime examples. Modifications to the core include using two different hardness lead cores for the front and rear of the core, the front being softer to enhance expansion and the rear being hard to halt it, as seen in the Speer Grand Slam bullet. Bonded-core bullets actually have the lead core soldered or electrochemically attached to the core, so that they cannot separate. This is often used in conjunction with tapered jacket thicknesses to control expansion. Many bullets, such as the Grand Slam, use combinations of these and other designs to improve the basic design. The small, sharp plastic tips so popular today help keep the bullet nose sharp for aerodynamic purposes, and also act as a wedge that drives back into the bullet core on impact, helping to initiate expansion. This is true of both the fragile varmint designs like the Hornady V-Max and Sierra Blitzking, as well as the Swift Scirocco and Nosler Ballistic Tip and Accubond big game bullets. Conversely, with the Hornady A-Max target bullets, the plastic tip is primarily there for aerodynamic improvement (though I believe Hornady considers their .30 caliber A-Maxes suitable for deer hunting).

Next we have the structural difference of a partition. This is basically a cup-and-core bullet with two separate cores, front and rear, divided by a solid wall of copper alloy that is integral to the rest of the jacket. Basically a copper rod is drilled from either end almost but not quite all the way through, and the cores inserted from front and rear. The partition acts as a positive stop to the expansion of the nose section core, allowing the rear of the bullet to stay intact and continue penetration after the front core has mushroomed. These are highly effective designs and well proven with the original Nosler Partition, which allows a generous nose section to mushroom enough to often lose most of its lead. Swift A-Frame bullets are similar, though apparently with the partition placed a bit more forwards to place more weight in the base and reduce expansion and weight loss of the nose core.

The Barnes X-bullet is quite a departure from other designs. Basically it is a solid slug of copper alloy with a carefully-designed hollow point hidden inside four carefully shaped separate nose petals that, upon impact, are driven to expand and peel backwards like four bent propeller blades. Considering that the bullet may be spinning upwards of over 200,000 RPM, that makes quite a roto-rooter going through some critter's chest cavity. Due to the design this bullet does not have a core that can separate, and it tends to retain its full weight unless one of the petals breaks off. The petal design both creates a terrible wound channel and allows very deep penetration, much more so than usual for the same bullet weight in a standard cup-and-core design. Due to the lighter weight of copper, X-bullets tend to be quite long to reach conventional weights for caliber. Too long of a bullet will require a faster than factory-standard rifling twist rate to stabilize it, which means that an all-copper bullet of the heaviest weight usually offered in a lead core bullet may not work in a given rifle, which is why you might not find X-bullets available at the heaviest weight for a given caliber that is offered for a standard lead core bullet.

The Winchester Fail-Safe bullet is essentially a cross between a partition bullet and an X-bullet. It has the X-bullet nose and a short lead core in the base. This allows for the bullet to be more of a standard length for its weight.

In terms of performance the standard cup-and-core bullet, even without any enhancements, fired from short action and standard cartridges such as the .243, .30-30, .308, .270, .30-06 etc. at normal ranges, still tends to work just fine on smaller to medium size game. If you want to plug your deer in the woods with your trusty .30-30 or .308, you don't need trick bullets.

If you think you need deeper penetration, most of the enhanced bullets have a reputation for holding together better, penetrating a bit more, and retaining more of their mass. The locked-core types, the bonded types, and the partition types will generally do a better job where an angling shot on a larger animal such as elk or moose is expected. These bullets also help the .243 perform better on medium-sized game.

The Barnes X and Winchester Fail-Safe bullets tend to have the deepest penetration and highest weight retention of all. The best use of these bullets is either for a large tough animal, or in a cartridge that would be considered a bit small for a given animal type. A .270 or 6.5x55 used on elk or moose, the .243 for large deer, mountain sheep, or goats, or any similar application will greatly benefit from these bullets in the heaviest weight available for caliber.

Earlier in the chapter I mentioned that it is preferable to have a bullet exit the animal rather than stopping inside its body. For years it has been a widely-held belief that a bullet that stops inside an animal delivers 100% of its kinetic energy, and therefore is preferable to one which exits and "wastes" some of its energy on the landscape beyond the target animal. While this is partly true – a bullet that stops inside does deliver 100% of its impact energy into the animal – it leaves unconsidered some important facts.

First, most things being equal – bullet diameter, construction, path through the animal's body, expansion diameter – a bullet that exits will make a longer wound channel and cause more bleeding, shock, and damage than one which stops well short of the animal's off side, and has potential for more blood trail on the ground from the exit wound.

Further, the reason that a bullet stops without exiting is that it did not have enough kinetic energy to keep overcoming resistance all the way through. As the bullet penetrates through the resistance of the animal's body, it gives up energy into the resistance as it overcomes it. Whatever energy it did have, is what drove it as far as it got. Look at it this way: If a given caliber bullet impacts, expands, and penetrates say three-quarters through an elk's body broadside, it took X amount of energy to drive it that deep, then it ran out of steam and stopped. Now think of a bullet of similar caliber bullet following the same wound path, with similar expansion, that drives all the way through. By the time this second bullet reaches the three-quarter distance where the first bullet stopped, it will have already transferred the same amount of energy as the first bullet that stopped there – it would have to in order to get that far. Yet, it keeps going through the other quarter of the elk's body width, delivering even more energy and creating a

longer wound as it does so.

If it does exit, so what – no matter how much extra energy it has that it takes with it, it has already dumped all the energy that it could have into the animal anyway, as the energy transfer takes place via the bullet pushing against tissue. So, because of the longer would track of the exiting bullet, it will actually dump more kinetic energy into the animal's body than one that leaves a shorter wound path (expansion diameter being equal).

The thing about this process is that given equal expansion (increased bullet frontal area, which generates increased resistance to penetration, and excepting for the moment the X-bullet advantage in penetration), for a bullet to exit as described above it must have greater impact energy than the one that stopped before exiting. So how do we get the extra energy? We get it through two means: either greater impact velocity or greater bullet momentum from greater bullet mass. The former can come from using a more powerful cartridge, taking a closer shot versus a farther shot, or perhaps using a higher B.C. bullet if we know must take longer than usual shots. The latter comes from choosing a heavier bullet with greater sectional density. Either way we are increasing the impact on the game animal. With the X-type bullets increased penetration is a design bonus, and with controlled-expansion lead core bullets it comes from smaller diameter expansion.

Either way, I believe that a bullet that makes a full penetration of the animal will provide for a more certain and probably quicker fatality than one which offers a shorter, shallower wound path.

Reading of things like shallow bullet blow-ups with the early high-velocity magnum rounds that caused wounded animals to run off, versus reading of the great success of such "slowpoke" old rounds like the .303 British with 215 grain controlled-expansion round nose bullets poking along at about 2200 fps achieving full lengthwise (not width!) penetration on large African beasts with attendant bang-flop effects, helps to illustrate what is going on here. A longer wound channel simply does more damage, and more damage, well, just has to really hurt more.

If you are going to decide on bullet type and weight for bigger game, it is in my humble opinion a safer bet to lean more towards deep penetration than towards high expansion.

The last point to mention is that all the "premium bullet" magic in the world won't help a bit if you don't deliver it with perfect accuracy. Bullet placement still comes before bullet performance. Learn where the vitals, skeletal structure, and desired aim point are on your intended prey from every angle before you go out hunting. Now go get some practice!

CHAPTER 15

DEALING WITH WIND

The simple fact of the matter is that for most big-game hunting inside 200 yards, you will have very little worry about the wind unless it is blowing so hard as to physically push you around (not just your bullet). But as ranges get past 200 and on towards 300 (and more so the further out you go), wind becomes something to which you have to pay attention.

The effects of wind can be calculated and are referenced in reloading manuals and ballistics programs, but always in terms of a "perfect" wind – that is, X miles per hour steady, at a 90 degree angle to your bullet's path, uniformly from your muzzle to the target.

Unfortunately, in the real world that seldom happens. When it does, be grateful, because what you otherwise get is a wind that shifts both speed and direction differently at different distances along your line of fire on a constant basis, mak-

Five shots from open-leg sitting with Ching sling at 200 yards. Three close shots fired first in no-wind condition, then wide low right and low left shots when fighting against a sudden strong gusting wind front that pushed me around. Black is eight inches wide, scoring rings are one inch wide.

ing it impossible to give more than a rough guess at what the "average" condition is at any given second. Being able to see and feel what the wind is doing at your position is one piece of information you need; being able to see which way the branches or grass are blowing at the target and at the halfway point are others.

Fortunately, as noted above you may never have to worry much about it if you are hunting in dense woods. On the other hand, if you are scanning across a 300 yard plowed field or sneaking up on a distant pronghorn antelope, you have to pay some attention to it.

First, you should already be aware of its direction as part of your scent-trail management as you hunt.

Second, you should develop some idea of whether it is below five miles per hour, around five, above five, around ten, above ten, and around fifteen or more. If you can feel it on your face, it's about three to five. Leaves in constant motion, six to eight or so. Small tree branches in constant motion, about ten. Large branches in constant motion, twelve to fifteen. Dorothy and Toto hurtling past thirty feet off the ground, time to go home.

Third, you need to pay attention to the patterns of both speed variations and direction variations.

Fourth, understand that a wind that is directly along your sight line to your intended target (either towards or away from you) is going to be something you can for practical purposes ignore, while a wind that is angled about 45 degrees to your line of fire will have about two thirds (not half) the value of a 90 degree crosswind. Winds at a shallow angle (from 11, 1, 5, or 7 o'clock relative to

the shooter) will have half the value of a ninety degree angle crosswind.

Finally, you look at the cheat sheet taped to the side of your rifle stock where you wrote what that reloading manual or ballistics program said that a 10 mph 90 degree crosswind will do to your bullet at various ranges and apply the appropriately adjusted component of correction based on the actual angle and speed of the wind and estimated distance to the target. Ha! You think I'm joking? Nope.

One of the things to take advantage of is that available info from loading manuals, ballistics charts, or online ballistics programs. Another is that the effect of wind is in direct relation to wind speed, so that if all the info you have for deflection is based on a 10 mph crosswind, you can calculate the deflection for a five mph crosswind as being half that of the 10 mph crosswind, and that for a 20 mph crosswind as being double that of the 10 mph crosswind. Factoring in the effect of more shallow wind angle as described above is another help. With this info and a fairly keen eye towards what is happening between you and your target, you can make a fairly decent guess at what to do.

Another gem of wisdom can be found in the WWII Army training film "Rifle Marksmanship with the M1 Rifle, Part 2" available for downloading from the internet. It explains rule-of-thumb methods for determining wind velocity and minute-of-angle click adjustments for the sights on the mighty M1 rifle. For estimating wind speed, take a piece of dry grass or a dry leaf and drop it from shoulder height. Point your arm straight from the shoulder at where it landed. The angle between your arm and your body, divided by four, roughly equals wind speed in miles per hour. Then, take the range to your target in hundreds of yards (300 yards becomes "3"), multiply it by wind speed in miles per hour, then divide that result by 10 (a constant derived from the wind drift resistance of a 150 grain military bullet fired from a .30-06 M2 cartridge). The answer gives you minutes of angle of windage compensation for the above round with a 90 degree crosswind, correctable for other wind angles as described previously. Other rounds may vary (the current military 5.56 round requires division by 7 since it drifts more), but you get the idea.

Let's look at some calculated wind deflection of common cartridges at 100, 200 and 300 yards just to have an idea of how much deflection distance we might see.

Once again retreating to my trusty 3rd Edition "Sierra Rifle Reloading Manual," we find that the proverbial perfect crosswind at 10 mph blows a .30 150-grain spitzer flat base bullet at 2900 fps (.30-06 speed) sideways .79 inch at 100 yards, 3.32 inches at 200 yards, and 7.81 inches at 300 yards. For a .30 180-grain spitzer flat base at 2700 fps (also .30-06), we have drift numbers of .77 inch at 100 yards, 3.18 inches at 200 yards, and 7.45 inches at 300 yards. Boattail bullets will reduce these numbers by about 10% to 18%, more so for the heavier bullet.

Notice that these numbers round out to less than a minute of angle at 100 yards, roughly 1.6 minute of angle at 200 and roughly 2.5 or so MOA at 300. Also of interest is that the 300 yard wind drift is approximately ten times (in inches) that of the 100 yard drift. According to my Sierra manual this latter is a very consis-

Drop dry grass or leaves from shoulder height.

tent phenomenon throughout the range of bullets and velocities, even at different wind speeds. Another consistent phenomenon the manual relates is that the 400 yard drift is about 85% more than the 300 yard drift. This latter bit makes for a handy calculation in the field, if you already know your 300 yard drift.

For the .270 with a 10 mph crosswind, we have the 130-grain boattail at 3000 fps having .64-inch drift at 100, 2.69 inches at 200, and 6.35 inches at 300. The 150-grain boattail at 2800 fps drifts .65 inch at 100, 2.75 inches at 200, and 6.44 inches at 300 yards. Again, well under one MOA at 100, less than 1.5 MOA at 200, and just over two MOA at 300.

Slower cartridges, like the .308-based rounds, will have more drift than the above rounds (perhaps 10% more), and magnum cartridges will have perhaps 10% to15% less.

As you can see, for these two popular

Point at where it landed with arm straight. The angle between your pointing arm and your body, divided by four, is wind speed in miles per hour.

becomes a waste of ammunition very quickly, whereas cranking in a specific amount of scope adjustment gets you the number you want every time (whether it's the number you actually need, now, is a different story!) and allows for a dead-on hold.

Appleseed teaches what we call "Fred's Simplified Wind Rule": for a noticeable breeze (approximately 10 mph), hold one minute of angle into the wind for every 100 yards distance to your target. This is designed to keep you in the black of an Army "D prone" target, which is about 26 inches wide by 19 inches tall. This is a much wider target than the vital zone of a big game animal, but is a fair starting point for experimentation.

Also, remember that a five mph true crosswind will have half the effect related above, a 20 mph wind will have double the effect, and a 45 degree angle wind will have about two-thirds the effect of a 90 degree crosswind. Winds that change direction between you and the target should have less effect than a pure crosswind – if the direction change is to lesser angle or reverse direction. If it changes direction from a 45 degree crosswind to a 90 degree crosswind, well, that makes matters worse. Winds that swirl, reverse, and fishtail back and forth will have, umm, a severe negative effect on your sanity. As you can see the real world will throw you curves that are quite difficult to decipher. This is why long range shooting is so difficult. The margin of error becomes quite tiny. Remember this when you are tempted to take a long shot when the wind is up. Targets are one thing, live animals are another – if the wind is troublesome, try to

cartridges in a 10 mph crosswind, you can ignore the effect out to perhaps 150 yards and apply Kentucky windage (aiming into the wind) of two or three inches at 200 yards. At 300 yards you have to be a bit more careful in judging wind and hold-off distance, as errors in judgment might put you out of the desired impact zone. This is where some experience on the target range in blustery conditions can pay big dividends. For most such situations between 150 to 300 yards, adding one to two minutes of angle of hold-off into a moderate wind will get you close enough to your desired impact point to do the job on even an antelope-sized animal.

For those of you shooting at little critters like prairie dogs, it is wise to crank the scope knobs for windage corrections, especially past 300 yards. Trying to guess at ten or fifteen (or more) inches of hold-off on a four-inch-wide target

Five shots from prone with Ching sling at 300 yards, with varying crosswind speeds during shot string.

tion against the force of the wind. Winds in the 15 mph range or greater will definitely push you around – even in a good solid sitting position with a tight sling – and only 10 mph of wind will make offhand shooting more difficult. Those of you fortunate (?) enough to have had the experience of fighting the wind at 600 yards in highpower bullseye competition will know what I mean when I say that you can't beat actual experience (the experience often beats you instead).

Wind-doping is what "separates the men from the boys" in long-range target shooting. For big game hunting within ethical distances (within 300 yards for competent shooters by my reckoning), it is less critical but still needs your attention.

stalk to within 250 yards or less of your quarry. Both you and the animal may regret it otherwise.

Don't stay home from the range on a windy day. Even if you're shooting from a bench, working against crosswinds at distance is quite educational. When shooting from position, you may find you have to use the next steadier position that the one you might ordinarily pick, just to increase the stability of your posi-

I suggest buying an inexpensive wind gauge such as the Caldwell Wind Wizard, sticking a 10-inch paper plate to a wide target backer, and going out shooting on a windy day. Get a feel for measured wind speed and its drift effect at different distances. Even a basic understanding of wind and its effect will be invaluable in the field. Don't forget to take it into account.

CHAPTER 16

THE ETHICAL LONG-RANGE HUNTER

This is a topic I almost hesitate to include, since I will most certainly come off to some people as preachy or snobbish. Unfortunately it is a topic I feel needs addressing, as there are a great many people operating under misapprehensions in the field with some resulting very ill effects on the game animal population.

My concern is with the apparently widespread notion that it is okay to blast away at animals at ranges out at a quarter mile or more. This notion pops up regularly in the gun press, often in tandem with a review of the latest Thunderwhacker magnum round that shoots flat halfway to Mars.

My own experience with shooting from 300 yards to 600 yards, informally with scoped big-game hunting rifles out to perhaps 420 yards (my longest available known distance range), in formal bullseye competition with an iron-sighted M1 Garand out to 600 yards, and chasing prairie dogs with a varmint rifle out to nearly 600 yards, has shown me just how easy it is to shoot a bad shot at these distances even under the best of circumstances. While I do not shoot these distances regularly with a standard big game rifle, I consider myself fairly decent at it – on paper or steel targets – but also fully aware of all the pitfalls associated with it. Paper, especially, shows you the blunt truth of just where your bullet actually went. It is easy to forget the six or ten misses you had before you hit that target way out yonder. This is especially so with people who never really had the chance, or made the effort, to really do a lot of work at long range. Even shooting prairie dogs from a steady bench, with a flat-shooting sub-MOA rifle, past 350-400 yards will clue you in real fast to the vagaries of the wind and the difficulties of range estimation.

It is easy to form an opinion based on limited exposure to something, especially when that exposure shows only one side of the issue. Having spent several years competing against highpower bullseye riflemen who could shoot nearly perfect scores from prone on a seven-inch ten ring at 300 yards and on a twelve-inch ten ring at 600 yards (with iron sights no less), it almost becomes expected that this kind of shooting is common, since most of the top dogs – at a highpower

match - can approach this (no, I'm not one of them). The guys who can shoot a 197 out of 200 at 300 yards prone rapid fire, and shoot a 195 out of 200 at 600 yards prone slow fire with the wind switching back and forth, can probably hit anything they want to at any range, and I have no problem with them trying – they really are that good, and prove it every time they show up on the line for a competition. They not only know what they are doing, they know how to figure out something they don't already know, and do it right.

Yet when observing the "regular guys" who show up at the range for a bit of bench shooting, their lack of skill can be a rude awakening. Most of the "regular guys" I have observed have never left the bench, and most of those that I have seen shooting from position have an effective range of about 100 yards on a deer-sized animal. From prone.

The sad fact of the matter is that the high-end competitors or long-range specialists are about one or two percent of the total rifle-toting population. Even the middle-level competitors (my slice) are about four percent, if that. Everyone else can be divided into the somewhat to fairly competent (perhaps 15-20%) and those who are well below that level (the other 75 or 80%). It is the thinking of the 95% of non-experts/masters that concerns me, because it is swayed by a combination of (in my opinion) irresponsible magazine articles and lack of personal experience.

Why does this bother me? What concerns me? When you miss the paper or steel mark, no harm done, but a near miss on an elk's kill zone may mean that instead of the shot hitting the lungs, it hits the guts or a leg. Now you have a wounded animal that can still run or hobble off to die a miserable death, at a distance so far you might not have a clue whether you hit it or not, and might not even be able to find the exact spot on which the animal was standing so as to look for a blood trail.

What I am talking about is ethical hunting behavior. This, unfortunately, does not necessarily have a common definition on which we can all agree, and there are plenty of hunters who never even give the matter much thought. See fur? Then shoot! Never mind how far, can't get 'em if you don't shoot at 'em, right? I guess something like that was going through the mind of the man I once saw firing shots (from standing) at a pack of antelope running about forty miles an hour about a quarter of a mile away.

We owe the animals we hunt as quick and clean a death as possible. If we care about this at all (and we should), then that means being about 95% certain of our shot placement. At least, that's what it means to me. And that 95% certainty must not just be an ego-stroking, self-serving assumption, but rather the knowledge that 95 of the last 100 shots we fired, in realistic training that accurately reflects what we must do in the hunting field, went right where they were supposed to go. You fire one shot at the animal, you hit its heart or lungs, it falls over dead. Period. End of story. Ninety-five times out of one hundred. And that goes for each and every variety of shot that presents itself, from a fifty-yard off-hand snapshot to the one way out there taken from prone over a rest.

The problem is twofold: there are

CHAPTER 17

PRACTICE DRILLS

Now that we know what to do, how do we practice it? We must start with the foundations and progress from there: gun mount and cheek weld, sight alignment/sight picture, correct position, loop sling, natural point of aim, trigger management, and finally developing our mental fire-control computers: applying these skills in situations where we have to make decisions and solve problems in the shortest time possible. Keep in mind, our marksmanship skills will be of little use if we cannot make correct snap judgments in the field regarding range estimations, specific aim point, wind reading, choosing the correct position, and our own capabilities/limitations.

Remember that the primary purpose of your training is to hit a big game animal's kill zone quickly out to 300 yards with your first shot with your centerfire rifle, or to hit a small game animal's kill zone quickly out to 100 yards or so with a rimfire. The overwhelming majority of your game shots ought to occur much closer than these limits.

So, this is your bread-and-butter skill zone. Working at longer ranges is fun and really helps perfect our skills and knowledge, but let's first concentrate on walking before running.

A very good practice aid is to obtain a .22 rimfire rifle of the same configuration and action type as your centerfire rifle, and shoot it extensively. Not only will this avoid developing a flinch reaction to recoil, but these days it will pay for itself in ammunition cost savings! If you can swing the money this will be one of the best skill investments you can make. What you do with the .22 will transfer directly to what you do with the centerfire in both marksmanship and manipulation of the action.

First, you must make sure you really know the fundamentals of sight usage, gun mount to cheek and shoulder, and trigger management. These are things best initiated either at the range from the shooting bench with either a .22 rimfire with live ammo or by dry-firing a centerfire, or at home in prone dry-fire, to avoid the distractions of a wobbly rifle and recoil. Get totally correct, comfortable, and familiar with the concept of having your eye properly centered behind the iron sights or the scope, and with the cor-

Getting your gear ready for the hunt is fun. But are your skills ready?

rect cheek weld to stock comb that puts your eye in the right place, and the correct position of the butt in your shoulder to get you the correct cheek weld. Next, learn to get a surprise break every shot, whether live .22 rimfire or dry centerfire. Watch your sights; they should never move when the striker snaps, and you should truly never be able to anticipate exactly when that moment comes. This will be a bit dull and boring, but make sure you have this down pat; without these basic skills, you will never progress beyond the beginning stage. Remember, the whole point of getting a steady position is to be able to put these aiming and trigger skills to their best use.

Next, in learning the various positions, you should at first practice each of them at home in dry-fire. This will pay great dividends before you spend time and money traveling to the range and firing live ammo, and you can do it rain or shine, night or day. I suggest you start with the prone position as it is the steadiest, and work upwards from there – sitting, kneeling, squatting, and then standing.

Teach them while they're young. Note the girl readying the GI web loop sling.

A little sibling rivalry between my friend's children. Note the web loop sling on the girl's arm. The young man left his at home.

SAFETY WHILE MOVING

One note on safety needs to be stressed here. When transitioning from standing ready to any position, and then moving from position back to standing ready again, KEEP THE MUZZLE IN SAFE DIRECTION AND YOUR FINGER OFF THE TRIGGER!! It is terribly easy to wave the rifle all over the place when transitioning into or out of position, especially when getting back up on your feet. Keep control of the muzzle direction!

Learn to do this when dry-firing on the living room floor. It won't matter so much when you are all alone out in the woods getting up, but at the shooting range, you'll want to keep the muzzle downrange towards the target and not sideways at your fellow shooters!

Ingrain this habit while dry-firing at home. This is extremely important! Also, in standing ready the rifle's safety should be on, and your thumb on or near it. Don't move the safety to off until you are in the position. When you leave the position to stand up, the first thing you do is put the safety on before you get up.

THE COMPLETE DRY/LIVE FIRE DRILL

It is worth putting on some padding when doing long sessions of position practice. The loop sling will pull very tight against the back of your upper arm, the forward sling swivel will dig into your hand, and the buttstock will grind your shirt into the skin of your shoulder. A light jacket or roomy hooded sweatshirt (the kind with a lining) ought to be enough, along with a thin leather glove on your support hand. Leave the jacket un-zipped to allow freedom of move-ment getting into and out of position. If you are live-firing a centerfire rifle of about .270 or larger in size for any decent amount of rounds, you'll want to replace the factory "rubber brick" recoil pad with something like the Kick-Eze or Limbsaver super-soft types. If you're shooting a thumper like a .30-06 or a magnum, then you'll probably want one of those wimpy shoulder pads too. Yes, I know, you're big manly stud and recoil doesn't bother you. But when you start missing three or four in a row, and they all go to the support-hand side of the target, and you realize that you didn't see your sight lift in recoil, and so you dry fire a couple snaps and see your crosshairs jerk over to the support-hand side of the target, you'll realize that your shoulder is bucking in anticipation of recoil as you're squeezing the trigger, and old Pete knew (from experience) what he was talking about.

Oh, and the barrel of your centerfire rifle will get very hot, very quickly. Five or so quick rounds will warm it up nicely, and as you continue it will get burn-you hot in short order. Hence the recommendation above for a glove on the support hand. Give the barrel a rest every few rounds to cool, and also to let you work the kinks out of your limbs.

When dry or live firing, work in this order:

FIRST, acquire your position and perfect it, including making sure the sling loop length is set correctly (as short as possible!), and checking all steady hold factors (SHF's).

SECOND, relax both mind and body as much as possible. Sag into the sling and let it do the work.

THIRD, adjust your NPA to be on

target at the end of normal exhalation (natural respiratory pause). Remember the "close eyes, relax, inhale, exhale, hold, open eyes" drill for checking NPA. Remember if you find yourself "trying" hard, something's wrong! The first three steps above should do the work for you, if you perform them properly. If you're working hard to aim the rifle and hold it steady, go back and re-check them. Position shooting is not comfortable, but it should be a very minimalist activity.

Your correct position, sling usage, and natural point of aim form the three-legged stool of relaxed steadiness. One leg missing and the stool tips over.

FOURTH, focus your eyes and mind intently on your sight picture (get in the "bubble"). If using iron sights, be certain of correct sight alignment and intense front sight focus; if using a scope, look at the intersection of the crosshairs, not the target. Keep the sight on the target at your chosen aim point. Let the rifle wobble; just use NPA to center your wobble zone on your aim point. If you are having difficulty with this, re-check your NPA, re-evaluate your position steady hold factors, see if you can tighten up (shorten) the sling loop any further, and stay as relaxed as possible. Remember that you must evaluate your sight picture and NPA at the respiratory pause between exhale and inhale. This is the point in your breathing cycle where you will be pulling the trigger.

FIFTH, when you have your small wobble zone centered on the target, proceed with a steady correct trigger press at your respiratory pause. Don't push on the stock with your trigger finger, and don't move or squeeze the rest of the hand.

Get the surprise break; keep your mind relaxed and resist the urge to snatch at the trigger when things look perfect. This last is a terribly bad habit; if you have it, you must break it! Just shoot within your wobble zone and accept where the hit goes! This sounds counter-intuitive, but it does work; don't try to fuss the shot or fire deliberately at a given instant. You should be able to get the shot off in no more than four or five seconds, before you need to inhale again (remember you'll be in motionless respiratory pause). As you get better this time frame will shorten. A three to four second cadence is what is considered rapid fire, or "rifleman's cadence". If the shot doesn't want to happen, take a breath and start over. Remember that this process is enabled by your NPA being on target; your

The target-shooter offhand stance. Taught to her by her father, the state 2005 offhand champion.

sights will return to the target all by themselves after recoil. Once you accomplish this, almost all your shots can be taken at this cadence; there is no need to go slower since NPA will do the aiming for you. The exception will be shots fired at extreme ranges, say past 400 yards; you'll want to be a perfectionist at those. Get your NPA aligned with the target and then trust it.

Good bolt work, from the shoulder, as it should be. "Shoot like a girl if you can," indeed!

SIXTH, follow through by keeping your head down on the stock and eye behind the sights, calling your shot (even a dry snap can be called; watch your sights!), seeing where the sight settled after recoil (a good quick NPA indicator), performing proper trigger reset (if shooting a semi-auto, don't slap your finger forward off the trigger), working a manual action without lowering the rifle, regaining your sight picture, and re-checking NPA.

These are the building blocks of an accurately fired shot. It is VITALLY important that you run this drill exactly. If you leave anything out your accuracy will suffer!

EVERY shot you fire in practice should run right down this list! Ingrain it as a habit. I know it sounds like a lot to do, but soon enough you will do it automatically, without thinking, and at a very high rate of speed.

THE MIND GAME

This is the hardest part. RELAX YOUR MIND! Stay positive, forget about the last shot, and work through your steps. Don't worry about the last shot or the next shot, focus on THIS shot. Don't think, don't "try", just shoot. You'll find that the harder you try, the worse you will do. So don't "try", just "do." Let the techniques and principles above do the work for you. When you execute correctly you will be surprised at how simple and effortless a steady hold right on your target can be. Clear your mind of impatience, desire, excitement, worrying about group size or accuracy, pride and ego, beating your shooting buddy, the last mistake you made, etc. All this is distracting, self-defeating mental and emotional junk! Work on your cold, focused "fire control computer". Hypnotize yourself with your sight picture into a sort of detachment from the process, and have fun. The ball and dummy drill mentioned in the chapter on trigger management is a big help to achieve this with live fire. Lots of dry fire has the same effect. Do it!

Take your time and work on every particular of each position, paying close attention to your body position details, the principles of position, SHF's, tight sling tension, your NPA, what you see in movement of your sights, and especially trigger action. Learn to completely relax both mind and body (this is extremely important!) Be sure of what you are trying to accomplish, analyze your position in every detail large and small, and when you think you are ready, shoot dry snaps carefully with repeated shots. Get a good surprise dry snap that your sight picture tells you would have hit. Perform as perfectly as possible. Keep track of the relative size of your wobble zone in each position, because this is the gauge of your skill. Your goal will be to shrink this with practice. Eventually you will memorize them for each position in minutes of angle. This is very important, as this will be the indicator of which position you will use to hit a given target size at a given range. Dry-fire each position extensively before switching to live fire.

When you are confident in what your sight picture shows you and in your construction of the various positions, this is the time to switch to live fire to confirm results. Pace your live sessions slowly at first, working on only one or two positions, firing at least 30 shots in each. Shoot a series of five or ten shot groups from position. Take your time and analyze what you are doing for each shot. Remember, each shot is a learning experience!

Note your position correctness, sling snugness, NPA, wobble zone size, call, and sight position after recoil recovery for every shot. It is from these details that you will learn.

Though I will reference timed drills below, keep this thought in the forefront of your mind: Accuracy is the measure of your progress! You must first develop consistent accuracy in all your shooting, from whatever position. Whether you are trying to shoot the smallest groups you can, or are simply trying to keep your shots in the 8" smallbore target's black (a deer's kill zone), the accuracy vs. speed requirements are the same – you must hit. Attempts at speed should be guided by accuracy results. Shoot only as fast as you can consistently hit. It is desirable to push yourself once you feel comfortable with the basics, but at first, limit your speed of the shot to the fastest consistent hit you can get.

I advise starting your position training with the prone position as it is the most stable (though least comfortable!). It will get you shooting tight groups in the least amount of time, which is a big confidence booster. Next, the sitting position. Sitting requires a good amount of thought and effort in the beginning in order to pick the best variant for your individual body structure, after which it requires much less work. It is also your bread-and-butter hunting position. So, once you have gotten comfortable with prone, split your time about evenly between prone and figuring out your sitting position at first. Once you are comfortable with your sitting position and are getting very good results with it, keep half your training in sitting and branch out into standing. Standing is the least stable and requires the most work of all. As you progress in the sitting postion, you will reach a point when you think you've gotten it nailed down. Then keep half your training in the standing position and start working on squatting and kneeling instead of sitting. After getting comfortable with squatting and kneeling, if you then construct your training sessions to be always half standing shooting and the other half taking turns with one of the other positions, that will be a good starting program. With sufficient practice you will begin to know how best to apportion your time amongst the various positions.

I suggest starting with five-shot groups. Remember to keep the butt in your shoulder, cheek on the stock, and eye on the sights when working the action. This will give you enough repetition for useful feedback without wearing you down too much at first. And speaking of feed back.....

SELF-DIAGNOSIS I: THE TALKING RIFLE

Believe it or not, your rifle talks to you all the time. It is telling you things about your shooting you need to know. It speaks through its sights, on which you should be focusing with your eye and concentrating with all your thought. What can your front sight or crosshairs tell you?

1) Whether or not you're focusing on it (iron sights – sharp, not blurry iron front sight)

2) Whether or not you have proper sight alignment (both irons and scope)

3) Whether or not you have proper sight picture

4) Whether or not your NPA is on target (before, and after shooting)

5) Your wobble zone in MOA (how good your position & sling use are)

6) Calling where the shot went (follow-through – where was your sight at the shot?)

7) Ranging device – military front sight width & height, crosshairs reticle shape

8) Elbow properly under the rifle (vertical, not diagonal, tracking while breathing)

9) Detect movement caused by flinching/bucking/jerking in dry fire/ball & dummy

10) Did you see your sight lift in recoil, or are you blinking and flinching at the shot?

Every one of the above things represents a potential error in execution. If you don't know what is wrong, you don't know what to fix – so listen to your sights!

SELF-DIAGNOSIS II: THE TALKING TARGET

When examining the results of your shooting, there is much to be learned. Group pattern and placement will tell you what you are doing wrong or right. The first things you should think about checking are the quality of your shooting position and proper sling loop tension. Then check NPA. The third thing you should check is the series of steps to fire the shot - sight alignment and sight picture, held breath after exhalation, eye and mind focus, trigger press, and follow through. Lastly make sure nothing has come loose on your rifle sights or action screws.

Let's look at some of the variations you'll see.

Too-large groups

Your group size will mostly depend on the wobble zone size of your shooting position. What you see in your sight movement should tell you what you are going to get on the target. Make sure your cheek weld puts your eye in the proper centered position with a scope, or if using irons, that your sights are perfectly and consistently aligned. Large wobble zones mean your position needs perfecting, the sling loop needs shortening, or you need to physically relax more (usually, all three).

Small improvements in each of these can mean huge improvements in stability! So, persist in your attempts to fine-tune every detail. For sitting and prone with the loop sling, you should work for total relaxation, especially of the support arm and hand, letting the tight sling do the work. Make sure your breath is held at exhalation and your trigger pull is not moving the rifle. As you shrink your wobble zone so will your groups shrink.

Another cause for large groups is focusing on the target instead of the crosshairs or front sight. If you are not paying close-focused attention on your sighting device, it can wander off for parts unknown without you realizing it. This is especially true for iron sights with a short front-to-rear sight radius distance, such as short-barrelled carbines and especially handguns. Maintain perfect sight alignment and make the front sight glow red-hot with the intensity of your focus!

Consistent pulling of the rifle off target in one direction, or the sights recovering from recoil somewhere other than your aim point, or having two distinct groups from one shot string, means your NPA is not coinciding with your target (your NPA is where the rifle wants to go). Make the necessary adjustment.

Wild shots

Unexplainable wild shots that you couldn't call may mean you are jerking the trigger or flinching. Make sure your press is gentle and the shot is a surprise. Seeing your sight lift in recoil tells you you're not blinking, which means you're probably getting a good surprise break and not flinching.

Vertical stringing

If vertical stringing ocurs, make sure the loop sling is not sliding down your arm. This will allow the rifle to drop. Also make sure your cheek weld and buttstock position in your shoulder is constant. If your eye or the buttstock is moving up and down, it can cause this. During a string of shots from position, the buttstock should be glued in place in your shoulder and your cheek should be glued in place on the stock.

Also, your breathing and breath-pause point could be irregular. As you breathe in and out, the rifle muzzle should move down and up in prone and sitting, vice-versa in standing. Make sure you use the same natural respiratory pause and the same size breathing cycle from shot to shot. The easiest point to have consistency is the natural end of a natural exhalation.

Horizontal stringing

Incorrect trigger manipulation can cause horizontal stringing. Make sure you are contacting the trigger with the center of the end segment of your finger, right across the middle of your fingerprint. Make sure you are pulling straight to the rear, and not pushing or pulling the rifle to the left or right. Make sure your trigger finger is not "pulling wood" by contacting the side of the stock. Make sure your whole hand is not squeezing along with the trigger finger. Also check your scope for mount/ring looseness or front sight for drifting sideways if it is in a dovetail groove type mount. Make sure your NPA is not to one side of the target.

Diagonal stringing

This can be a combination of the above factors for horizontal and vertical stringing, or, your support arm elbow is not directly under the rifle but off to one side, which lets the rifle tend to cant or sag to the opposite side at an angle or to move up and down with your breathing at a diagonal angle rather than the vertical. Another problem can be the support hand flinching away from the recoil impact of the forward sling swivel, or the trigger-side shoulder flinching against the buttstock in anticipation of recoil. Go through them and eliminate each as a cause. Remember that dry fire and ball-and-dummy are good for finding trigger and flinching issues.

Good group sizes, but centered off your aim point, in varying directions

If this is hapening, your NPA is not consistently aligned with your target aim point. Take special care to verify and adjust it at the beginning of every shot group, and do not do anything to change

or disturb it (but if you do disturb it, recognize such and re-align it). Remember, in any position you always "have" a natural point of aim. The trick is to find where it is and make it coincide with your desired aim point. Take the time to verify it for every single shot at first. This should become second nature and with practice and experience you will soon enter your position with your NPA alignment either good enough or excellent right off the bat. If you want to be both fast and accurate even on small targets at great distances, this is one of your necessary skills.

Small group consistently off center in same direction

By this time you may simply need to adjust your sights. Be aware that from one position to another your zero may shift slightly, so if you are going to move your sights to shift the group to center, make sure you do it from the position, and at the distance, you consider to be your "bread and butter" primary usage. For my hunting rifles I use open-legged sitting at 200 or 225 yards, with tight Ching sling, to get a final zero.

One shot out from the rest of the group

Often this is your first shot, before you get yourself into a proper cadence coordination of NPA, respiratory pause, and trigger press.

Try taking a "fake shot" (execute everything but don't pull the trigger) for your first shot in order to get yourself in the groove, so all following actual shots are executed the same way.

Small group centered on target

Congratulations! You're doing it right.

PUTTING IT ALL TOGETHER: FROM STANDING READY TO THE HIT

This is the skill set you really want: from standing ready to a fast hit from any position, with the ability to plant a second hit in no more time than it takes to inhale and exhale (while working the action), confirm aim, and press. When you think you have figured out each position correctly, practice acquiring it from standing.

Beginning with your rifle slung over your shoulder or held at standard ready (port arms with the butt against your hip and muzzle in your line of sight), go into each position (looping up in the sling if applicable) and fire one aimed shot. Your primary goal here is to get into a correct and solid position as quickly as possible, with as correct an NPA/target coincidence as possible from the get-go. This is the crucial skill which allows high speed from standing to hitting! So, remember to check NPA each time.

This is another skill best started with dry fire. Get a good surprise trigger break every shot. Also watch how the rifle recovers from recoil after your first shot; it should be very close to or right on your aim point. If not, adjust your position accordingly to bring your NPA onto your aim point. Once you can get into your desired position with very little NPA correction required and with the rifle recovering from recoil back on your aim point by itself, you've got it! This is the time to add firing a second shot. Remember to keep the butt in your shoulder, cheek on the stock, and eye on the sights if working the action while inhaling and exhaling (this maintains your sight alignment and your good NPA to which you recovered after your first shot!). Your second shot

(second hit!) should only take about 3-4 seconds with even a manual action from a good sitting or prone position. And remember that these times and accuracy standards are a foundation level. Greater speed and accuracy are attainable!

SPEED

When you are happy with the results at this point, now is the time to speed things up. The reason we train for speed is that we have very little control over how much time we have to make a given shot in the field. Even if we are sneaking up on an unaware beast out at 250 yards, the wind might shift suddenly and bring it our scent. We have no idea how much time the animal will give us, so we must not waste one second. This does not mean hurrying to the point of error, but rather performing every function we need to perform to make a good shot as quickly and efficiently as possible. When the animal is down for keeps, we will have plenty of time to admire it, appreciate the moment, congratulate ourselves, get the shakes, or whatever. Attend to business efficiently first.

The only way to find out your limits (or further them) is to exceed them – so go ahead and try. Make your speed gain come from accelerating your assumption of a steady position with correct NPA. But once you get your sights on the target, shoot carefully enough to get your hit. At first, don't try to rush the actual trigger press; rather, speed up what gets you to that point. Keep in control of your mind and your body; don't let haste ruin the moment. Eventually you will be able to accelerate the trigger work as well, but let that happen naturally from high repetition of practice and getting in the groove of correct NPA-respiratory pause-press the trigger, instead of forced hurry. Be patient!

Speed yourself up to where you start missing about one out of three or four and work at that speed and cadence until you can consistently and easily get ten-for-ten at that speed. Then speed up again. Remember, a good rapid-fire cadence for repeat shots on the same target is about three seconds per shot, once you get into position, with a shallow inhale-exhale-hold between each shot. Correct NPA will make this a snap since the sight will recover from recoil quickly right back to your aiming point!

SPEED AND ACCURACY STANDARDS FOR EACH POSITION

For the following, you will start from the standing ready position, then move into the shooting position with NPA check, then fire. This is a drill best practiced in dry fire at home first; work it hard before going to the range with ammo. Use an electronic shot timer or a friend with a watch to time you.

For standing, start with the smallbore target/paper plate at 25 yards. Allow about three seconds for a hit in the black. When you consistently achieve 100% hits, try 50 yards with about four seconds. When you achieve 100% hits here, try 75 yards with five seconds, then 100 with about six seconds. Then work for faster times and further distances. Figure you want to be able to hit that plate ten-for-ten at a distance of at least 100 yards and preferably 150 yards. Don't forget you can use the sling in loop or (non-Ching sling) hasty to steady yourself. As

a rule you should be able to shoot a five-shot group of about three or four inches from standing at 50 yards, double that at 100, without taking more than about four or five seconds per shot. Smaller is better of course, but this a good start. If you hunt small game with a .22, you'll want to skinny it down even more.

For kneeling and squatting, start at 75 yards and allow six seconds from standing ready. When you achieve 100% hits, move the target back to 100 yards, then after achieving 95% there try 150 yards, trying to beat seven seconds consistently. If you have a Ching sling practice looping up in it as you drop to position; it should cost you zero time to use it. With an M1907 or GI web, you can put it on either before or after you hit the position. Try these positions with and without the loop sling and compare your wobble zone. It will make you a believer in the loop sling, especially the Ching: besides adding steadiness, the Ching allows you to take advantage of the acquisition speed of these positions without delay.

For sitting, start at 150 yards, moving back to 200. From standing ready, work on your speed to eventually fire a hit in ten seconds or less. The loop sling is critical here to maximize the range of this position; it can add 75 to 100 yards of effectiveness. Work to achieve a wobble zone under four minutes of angle, three if possible. When you get good, play with it out to 300 yards and see what you can accomplish.

For prone, start at 200 yards, and see if you can eventually get your hit in 10-15 seconds from standing ready, if your mobility allows. Move to 300 and try for fifteen seconds, if your range facilities allow. Absolutely use the loop sling here, and try using a field-expedient rest as well. Palma rifle competitors shoot from prone with a sling (no rest) at 800, 900, and 1000 yards. A good prone position with a tight loop sling should give you a wobble zone approaching one MOA!

If the starting distances above prove too difficult at first, by all means start closer. If your shooting facility is limited to 100 yards, for sitting start with a six-inch target, then switch to a four-inch bullseye; prone, start with a four-inch bull and work to two inches. At 100, try for at most a 4-5-inch group from squatting/kneeling, 2.5-3.5 inches from sitting, and 2-3 inches from prone. If you can't move into position quickly enough to match the above times, do the best you can. There's something to be said for staying fit and flexible!

RECORDING YOUR PROGRESS

Keep a written record of your times and each position's wobble zone in minutes of angle in a notebook. Wobble zone is best measured at 100 yards using a target with one-inch grid lines on it, viewed through a scope sight with enough magnification to see the lines. These targets are commonly available. Without the grid, you'll have to use the size of whatever features are printed on the target to compare your wobble zone. With iron sights, you should use a round bullseye of a known size and give it your best guess. If the latter doesn't work well, go by your group size. Just remember that wobble zone and group size won't necessarily be the same thing. If you are shooting well, you will be able to avoid shooting at your widest wobble swings and your groups will be smaller

than your wobble zone. If you are shooting poorly, you may yank or flinch a shot well outside your wobble zone. I prefer to use wobble zone as a measure because that tells me just how well I am executing the principles of position and NPA. Remember: everything you do in practice is geared toward shrinking the wobble zone of every position.

Further uses of the notebook are to record what position you practiced, how many shots you fired, how your shot calls matched actual shot locations, what you did well, what you did poorly, what problem solutions you found, and what new things you learned. Keeping a record of each session will prevent you from wasting time on unproductive activities and help you focus your training far more efficiently.

GUARANTEEING A HIT?

When in the field, choose a position that easily keeps the wobble zone well within the kill zone of the animal. With a surprise trigger break, this virtually guarantees a quickly lethal hit! If this is not possible, either pick a more stable position or move closer (Col. Cooper's dictum "If you can get closer, get closer. If you can get steadier, get steadier").

With enough full-distance practice per above, you'll soon learn to match position to target size and distance. When in doubt, stalk as close to the animal as you dare, then shoot prone if possible, preferably over a rest. Remember, you owe the animal a quick clean death. Practice should show you just how far you have any business shooting at game. Forget all those stories you've read of the 600-yard elk shot. Brag instead about how close you stalked and how steady you held. Know your abilities and save the long-range stuff for paper, where you can learn about compensating for range estimation, trajectory drop, and wind drift without gut- or leg-shooting a live animal in the process.

It will take many hours of careful, attentive dry-fire and live-fire practice, but you can constantly improve your accuracy, consistency, and speed. Periodically re-run the Plate Drill and check your progress. If you can easily get all ten hits in a nice small group in a minute and a half or less, every time, you have reached a fair degree of competence. You can spice up the drill by adding a plate at 200 yards, and shooting five shots on each within the same time limit.

GUNHANDLING: KEEPING YOUR RIFLE RUNNING

By this I mean keeping your rifle in business in a very efficient manner. In the chapter on trigger management I mentioned working the action from the shoulder after firing a shot, while keeping your face on the stock and eyes on the sights. This saves lots of time and maintains your shooting position. Avoid the habit of firing a shot, lowering the rifle, and looking downrange. Don't think that you're finished after one shot. Another good habit to learn is quickly placing fresh rounds in your magazine. This is especially handy in running the drills above, as it will keep you going. Keep your spare rounds in an accessible pocket, in belt loops, or on a buttstock cuff on your rifle.

Get into the habit of quickly adding fresh rounds to the magazine whenever you have finished running a drill (lowering the rifle butt to your hip), or even when you are partway through a drill and still have some rounds left in the magazine (keep the butt in your shoulder in firing postition, top off with two or three rounds, and keep shooting). Learn to reload by feel with your eyes staying on target. Learn to keep track of how many rounds are in the magazine. Have a focused and businesslike attitude that keeps the rifle continuously in action.

Why? Remember, on the range you are in charge of your timing and cadence of fire, and there are few external time pressures beyond your control. It's very easy to become lackadaisical. However, once you get away from the range and out into the "real world" of hunting or battle, you are no longer in charge of time. Your quarry or your enemy will control target exposure and you will have to adapt to conditions beyond your control.

Bad habits from the range can cost you an opportunity in the field. I saw this when taking a friend on his first prairie dog shoot. He was set up on a shooting bench with his single-shot rifle on a rest, and selected a rodent to shoot. With his left hand he plucked a cartridge from its box which was to the left of his rifle. He transferred the cartridge from his left hand to his right. He laid it down on the rifle's follower and looked at it. He nudged it with his finger and looked at it again. He nudged it with his finger again, then closed the bolt, then settled in behind the scope.

By this time the prairie dog's sixth sense had sent it scurrying down his hole. My friend's bad habits had been formed on the shooting range where he could take all the time he wanted puttering around with every shot. I had to break him of those habits and get him to keep his cartridge box on the right side of the rifle and to load and close the bolt with one quick motion of one hand. Now of course we had other varmints at which to shoot, but imagine if that were a trophy bull elk vanishing into the brush? So, be quick to get into position and align your NPA, be quick to work the bolt, be efficient in all your movements, don't waste time or motion, keep the rifle shouldered and loaded. This is a mental attitude – part of programming your "fire control computer" - that takes some effort to obtain but it will pay great dividends in the field when time is short and opportunity fleeting. This is extremely important!

Hardened steel disk hanging from re-bar frame.

TARGETS

Once we get beyond the good old paper plates or smallbore targets, we might want to consider some others. Plates of hardened armor steel are excellent, if you keep the following in mind: their closest use with a centerfire rifle should be either the manufacturer's recommendation or about 150 yards, whichever is further! Bullets fragment on steel and pieces can come back at you! Also at 100 yards high velocity rounds such as the .223 can dimple even armor steel, beating up your expensive plate pretty quickly. The benefit of steel is primarily that you don't have to run down range and check your hit; it's a pretty audible whack. This saves lots of time. These are not group-size targets, they are hit-or-miss (pass/fail) targets, so choose the sizes according to your accuracy standards. Eight- to ten-inch squares or circles make a nice training target for big game.

One thing about steel is that you won't necessarily see where your miss went, so you lose the learning opportunity. This is where a well-developed ability to call your shot will help.

The use of soft scrap steel with a centerfire will be disappointing, since most modern rounds will punch right through it. Use hardened steel meant for rifle fire. AR400 or AR500 steel in 3/8-inch thickness works well. An internet search will turn up a number of target sources. I recently found snowplow blade edges of hardened steel at my local scrap yard. Thirty caliber full metal jacket bullets from a .30-06 just took off the yellow paint. Fortunately I had a pickup truck to fit the 160-lb. chunk, and a friend with a plasma cutter that could cut the thick steel into target-sized pieces. Cost? $60. The only reason I tried it was because it had the words "Heat Treated" stenciled on it.

Homemade deer targets can be cut out of large sheets of corrugated cardboard. I have found that making two and stapling them together in a double layer makes them survive the rigors of transport, storage, and high winds much better. Your imagination, art skill, and the size of the cardboard you can scrounge is your limit; deer, hogs, coyotes, antelope, full-size black and grizzly bears (yep got some of those!), Al-Qaeda terrorists....ahem.

Hand-drawn cardboard cutouts, paper plate, and 100-yd smallbore target.

Bambi turns to venison. Three separate one-shot standing-to-sitting drills at 200 yards, about eight seconds average for each one. The tape covering the wide left and right shot holes is why we all need to keep practicing.

He missed me, I didn't miss him. Three separate one-shot standing-to-squatting drills at 100 yards. I did throw one high into his rifle fore-end.

COMBINATION DRILLS

A great drill that tests your accuracy, speed, and ability to assume positions is the Rifle Bounce. Ideally, it is run with three steel Pepper Popper targets, though steel plates of around 10-12 inches in diameter may be used. One is set at 100 yards, another at 200, the last at 300. The drill is timed. The shooter starts at standing ready, and on signal is required to hit each target once. The 100-yard target must be taken from standing. Then the shooter must move sideways a step or two and engage the 200-yard target from the position of his choice.

Repeat the process for the third target. With steel targets the hit is audible, allowing the shooter to proceed to the next target. Time is unlimited, but the shooter is allowed only six shots. The time taken from start signal to the third target hit is the shooter's score. If you can hit all three in less than 30 seconds and have rounds to spare, you're doing okay. Twenty seconds with three shots indicates you know exactly what you are doing.

A variation of the rifle bounce is useful for learning the difference in your capabilities in the highest, fastest, and least steady positions: standing, squatting, and kneeling. Put up three paper targets at 100 yards. Starting from standing, fire three shots at the first target, then assume the squat and fire two at the second target, then assume kneeling and fire two more at the last target. No time limits, no worries about hitting one target before moving to the next, no need to move sideways between positions. This will give you a pretty good idea how these three quick-to-assume positions compare and help give you some notion

about the ranges at which you should use one versus another - programming your fire-control computer.

The snapshot at 25 and 50 yards makes an excellent drill all by itself. It combines the standing position, a perfect high speed gun mount with perfect NPA, and high speed of sight picture acquisition and trigger management. Making the 1.5 seconds par time is quite a challenge. The key is to get your NPA and mount perfected so that the crosshairs appear on or very near the target at first sight, as a form of learned muscle reflex.

Rifle Ten is a drill that requires a 300 yard (or meter) range on which a shooter can move forwards a distance of 100 yards. Five targets are set up at 300 yards. The targets are usually a practical "combat" silhouette of the IPSC or IDPA type, but you can be flexible here.

The shooter starts at this distance and fires two shots on the first target from prone. Then he advances 25 yards and shoots two shots at the second target from the position of his choice. This advance 25 yards and shoot two on the next target is repeated until the shooter fetches up at the 225 yard line for the fourth target. He must shoot this target from a position other than prone. And at the 200 yard line, the shooter must engage the fifth target from standing. The final tally is total points and total time. This is not easy to arrange on most shooting ranges, but it really puts the shooter to the test.

Another informal drill is shooting a single eight-inch smallbore 100-yd. target from varying positions and with varying time limits for a total of 50 shots, after which you score the well-perforated target. Ten individually-timed snapshots at 25 yards, ten consecutive standing shots at 75 yards in a single time of say three minutes, ten total shots at 100 yards from standing ready to either squatting or kneeling, shooting twice each on five individually timed attempts at 12 seconds each, ten consecutive shots at 200 yards from sitting in three minutes, and ten consecutive shots at 200 yards in prone in five minutes.

That will certainly give you a bit of a wringing out. If the time limits sound a bit short, just keep training until they seem luxurious. This drill, because of using the scoring rings for points, should emphasize accuracy skills over speed.

One drill that Col. Cooper thought was a good test is to run 200 yards downrange from the firing line, set up an eight-inch steel disk, run 200 yards back to the firing line, and knock over the disk with a bullet. Run 200 yards back out to set it up again and run 200 yards back to the firing line, and repeat for a total of five hits. I have never tried this one, but I can imagine it gives you some practice in settling yourself down!

Other games can help program your "computer" and challenge your decision-making speed. Set up targets at different ranges, if you can. Then have a shooting friend call out which one or more for you to engage, and in what order, starting from standing ready and changing from one shooting position to another as the target size and distance dictates.

Or, if your facilities allow, a vision barrier (tarp, sheet of cardboard, whatever) can be erected behind which a shooter stands (without rifle). A friend goes downrange and sets up an array of targets at different distances. On his return the shooter, still behind the vision barrier (but ok'ed by the friend) can then load and safety-on his rifle while facing downrange. Then the barrier is pulled aside (or the shooter steps aside) and the shooter engages what he sees, near-to-far, as quickly as possible. The combinations are as varied as your imagination, facilities, and safe shooting allow. Remember what you are trying to test and always be extremely careful in the design and performance of any such events, both as to gunhandling and line-of-fire.

Something to keep in mind is that while you can develop very good position skills on the flat floor of your living room or range firing line, when you get out in the field the ground will be much less accomodating. You will have to learn to adapt to sloping and uneven ground, grass and brush, rocks, etc. See if you can find a place to practice that allows such variations.

Remember to always keep in mind the specific goal of each training session. Pick a skill set or two, study its requirements ahead of time, work them in dry practice at home, and only then focus on these at each range session. The most important shot is the shot you are in the process of firing. Learn from each one and if you have a bad shot, learn its lesson, don't get frustrated, and make the next shot perfect. Keep a notebook of your sessions to record problems, solutions, ideas, and progress. Keep at it and the attainment of expert-level skill will be only a waypoint on your journey to mastery!

CHAPTER 18

COMPETITION AND PROFESSIONAL TRAINING

Why professional training? Simply put: There is no substitute for a qualified coach to watch over you. You will learn new things and break bad habits faster this way than any other.

PROFESSIONAL TRAINING & SHOOTING SCHOOLS

The Appleseed Project (www.appleseedinfo.org) I have recently come across this relatively new, non-profit, all-volunteer endeavor sponsored by the Revolutionary War Veteran's Association. Their purpose is to reawaken Americans to their cultural heritage, to remind us of the sacrifices that led to our freedoms, and to carry on the tradition of every American being a rifle marksman.

The Appleseed Project combines an intense two-day weekend rifle marksmanship clinic with the story of what happened on April 19th 1775. On this day the British soldiers marched out from Boston to seize the military stores of the Massachussetts colonials, Paul Revere made his famous ride, and the "shot heard 'round the world" was fired - starting the Revolutionary War. The instruction and curriculum of the rifle training is first-rate and the stories of what happened that day will remind you of just

what great sacrifices were made by the founders of this country. And the cost is almost negligible, especially when compared to similar instruction almost anywhere else.

Their website is www.appleseedinfo. org. The schedule of events can be found on the home page, and the forum will have the operational information, where you can ask questions of the cadre in your state.

Appleseed instruction encompasses all of the critical fundamentals of rifle shooting, condensed into a series of steps that is taught efficiently on Saturday and reinforced through repetition on Sunday. It teaches you the right techniques and habits and helps break your bad ones. Its all-volunteer (unpaid) instructors go through a rigorous, multi-step progression of training in how to instruct marksmanship and run the event, from four levels of "Instructor in Training" to "Full Instructor," then to "Shoot Boss," then "Senior Instructor," then "Master Instructor."

Shooters are instructed in safety, position, natural point of aim, sling use, concepts of minutes-of-angle and sight adjustments, rapid fire, and the mechanics of firing an accurate shot (sight alignment, sight picture, respiratory pause, focusing eye on the front sight and mind on keeping the sight on the target, trigger squeeze, and follow through) Saturday morning and early afternoon.

The course of fire is based on the instruction program used by the military in the early and middle twentieth century, which was far more comprehensive than that taught today. All Saturday shooting is done at 25 meters to first get people on paper, second get a zero easily, and third to waste as little time as possible going back and forth from line to targets.

(insert picture 5828 here: This young man sports an Appleseed shirt. The young lady has earned her Appleseed "Rifleman" patch.)

When the students have reached a certain level of proficiency, they will be introduced to the Appleseed version of the Army Qualification Test, scaled down to be shot at 25 yards.

This is four stages: standing slow fire, 10 shots in 2 minutes on one target simulating 100 yards; sitting rapid fire, 10 shots including a reload on two targets in 55 seconds, simulating 200 yards; prone rapid fire, 10 shots including a reload on three targets in 65 seconds, simulating 300 yards; 10 shots prone slow fire in five minutes on four targets simulating 400 yards, which counts double. If the shooter can manage a 210 out of 250 points (roughly Army "Expert" class), he or she will be awarded a nice embroidered patch that says "RIFLEMAN" and, if they so desire, will be invited to become a volunteer instructor with the program.

On Sunday, if range facilities allow, the students with centerfire rifles will be taken to whatever full-distance range is available (depending on the host range) to see that what works at 25 meters also works at longer distances, and to learn about zeroing, sight elevation come-ups, and wind compensation for different distances. At many ranges, facilities allow the rimfire .22 shooters to move to 100 yard targets to experience the same.

At this time the cost to attend an Appleseed is ridiculously low. If you sign up on the website ahead of time, they charge adult males $80 for two days and $50 for one day; adult females $40 for two days, $20 for one day; youth less than 18 years old $20 for two days, $10 for one day or one free youth per paying adult. Law enforcement officers and active or reserve/National Guard military are free.

Walk-ons without pre-registration may be charged $5 more per day. The private club range that hosts the shoot will usually charge another few dollars per day per shooter, usually about $5-10/day in my neck of the woods.

The standard to which they teach is the World War II military standard of shooting four minutes of angle or better with a rack-grade military rifle and military ammo, to allow for a hit on an enemy soldier out to 500 yards. They also offer a "Rifleman's Boot Camp" which is a full week course culminating in a weekend Appleseed shoot, for a very reasonable price, roughly about $200.

If you are looking for comprehensive rifle instruction for a very low price, Appleseed fills the bill far better than anything else I have seen. The skill sets taught are adaptable to any kind of shooting and thus jive well with the direction and content of this book. And the history of our nation's beginning is a bonus (well, actually, it's the main purpose of the program). The program is putting out roots nationwide, opening eyes, hearts, and minds everywhere with its stories of the "shot heard 'round the world" and spreading the fundamental skills . I myself was sufficiently impressed with the program to have joined up and have worked my way up to full instructor and shoot boss status. I encourage you to find the nearest one and attend.

Schools

There are a number of established shooting schools which offer intense and comprehensive training in the practical uses of rifle, shotgun, and pistol for various purposes. These classes range from two or three days to five days.

The Gunsite Training Academy in Prescott, Arizona, founded by the late Col. Jeff Cooper in 1976 (at first called the American Pistol Institute), is probably the oldest and the one that set the standard for all that followed.

Thunder Ranch (formerly in Texas, now in Oregon), run by Clint Smith (a former operations manager for Gunsite) runs a similar curriculum, and is widely considered the best shooting school in the world.

Both of these schools run a wide variety of classes from general to highly specialized with all sorts of firearms. There are other schools as well, such as Tom Russell's American Firearms Academy, Chuck Taylor's American Small Arms

Academy, Jim McKee's Shootrite Academy, Ron Avery's Practical Shooting Academy, and Dr. Ignatius Piazza's Front Sight Institute.

From the rifle perspective, the General Rifle 1 course referenced in Chapter 1 is offered by both Gunsite and Thunder Ranch, and is the fundamental hunting rifle course which corresponds with the material in this book. Above and beyond that, there may be a General Rifle 2 course which requires a higher performance level from the student, long-range shooting courses appropriate to military snipers, urban combat rifle courses oriented (but not limited) to military and law enforcement, specialty courses dealing with firearms of the Old West or early 20th century military arms, and others.

Defensive Shotgun (in the self-defense mode) and various defensive handgun courses are also prevalent. Investigation of these schools' websites will show what is currently offered. There are also a number of individual trainers who will come to your location. It pays to do some research to find out who is good. This is where hanging around competition shooters can come in handy.

My own experience with these is limited to one General Rifle and one General Pistol class run by Col. Cooper. They were well worth every cent, in particular the pistol class, where I learned more in five and a half days than I had learned in literally twenty years of puttering around on my own! Between the material taught and the watchful eyes of good instructors, the students will come out far ahead of where they were when they went in.

They are not cheap, and the pacing of the classes can be quite intense at times, though the instructors are always helping you along. Next to an Appleseed, in no way can you learn more in less time – as long as you pick the right school or instructor – and the difference between an untutored student on the first morning and the graduate will be an order of magnitude. If you can spare the time and money such a school (after attending an Appleseed event) will be one of the best skill investments you can possibly make.

Even if you plan on attending one of these professional schools for rifle, I would absolutely recommend attending a local Appleseed first. Not only because it will be much cheaper (a school might cost $1000-1500 for a five-day course, vs. an Appleseed weekend being anywhere from about $90 to $10!) and much less travel (there's probably an Appleseed shoot within a four hour drive from you), but it will give you comprehensive grounding in all the fundamentals so that when you show up at the expensive shooting academy you'll have a good understanding of principle, no bad habits, and be able to do well enough at the start to max out your training there. And I should point out that some schools may not come near Appleseed in drilling in the foundational skills, principles, and techniques.

Army training films

In WWII the U.S. Army made training films on everything under the sun, including marksmanship. "Rifle Marksmanship with the M1 Rifle", Parts 1 and 2, are on the internet and can be downloaded free. Part 1 is a truly excellent and fairly comprehensive tutorial on marksmanship fundamentals (it leaves out a bit on aperture sight alignment and sight picture) to 500 yards, and Part 2 explains zeroing, trajectory, wind reading, and sight compensation. With only a couple of small changes (notably the prone position), these fundamentals of accurate and rapid fire have remained unchanged to this day. And they're free!

COMPETITION

Next to professional training, the best thing to get you learning faster and learning better is engaging in some form of competition. Here you will get to mix with some very accomplished shooters, who are usually quite willing to share their expertise with newcomers. And shoot while a whole bunch of other people are watching, too! While the concept can be quite forbidding to some people, and some forms of competition require highly specialized (and expensive) equipment (either to be competitive or to conform to the rules), you should undertake every effort to find out just what sorts of competitions are held in your area. Not all have such stringent requirements. Even showing up to watch and talk to some of the shooters allows you to learn quite a bit, at no risk to your self-image.

The formal types of competition are quite well established. Let's start with bullseye target shooting. NRA Smallbore Rifle is done with a .22 rimfire at ranges out to 100 yards. It is timed position shooting and uses standing, kneeling, sitting, and prone.

International Shooting Union (ISU) Smallbore is similar, with slightly different targets and rules. Both of these disciplines use quite specialized and sophisticated rifles and equipment.

The stiff jacket helps stabilize the body in offhand, and the padded shoulder, elbows, and loop sling area, as well as the mitt, help the other positions be more comfortable.

NRA Highpower Rifle is done with a centerfire rifle, at ranges of 200, 300, and 600yards. It too is position shooting, using standing slow fire without sling at 200 yards, sitting (or kneeling, but no one kneels unless they can't sit) with sling rapid fire at 200 yards, prone rapid fire with sling at 300 yards, and prone slow fire with sling at 600 yards.

On a proper highpower range, the targets are set on frames that can be raised from or lowered into a trench or pit below ground by those competitors not engaged in either shooting or marking the scorecards for those that are. Everybody takes turns shooting, scoring, or pulling targets. Target pullers put a spotter disk in the bullet hole and another disk at a specific position around the frame perimeter corresponding to the score of the shot, so the shooter and scorer can see

them through their spotting scopes.

In slow fire the shooter loads and fires one shot, with a time limit of one minute per shot, then the puller lowers and marks the target and runs it back up. In rapid fire the shooter loads a specified number of rounds depending upon rifle type (five rounds for a "match rifle" – usually a bolt action, and two rounds for a "service rifle" – an M1, M1A/M14, or AR15), starts from the standing position with sling on arm, and then goes into position when the targets come up out of the pits. The first load of ammo is fired, the rifle reloaded with five rounds for match rifle and eight for service rifle, and the rest of the shots are fired all within a prescribed time limit (60 seconds for 200 yards, 70 seconds for 300 yards).

Targets are then pulled and marked after the time limit is up. The 50-shot

A hand-built, match-accurized Springfield M1A with stainless steel heavy Krieger match barrel, fiberglass stock, and National Match sights. Underneath is a hand-made Creedmoor shooting jacket.

Sixty seconds to get from standing to sitting, shoot two, reload, and shoot eight, at a seven-inch 10-ring at 200 yards. Your NPA has to be on target, your eye focus on the front sight, and your shooting in rifleman's cadence to get a good score.

Another X! (Yeah, sure.)

National Match Course comprises two slow fire sighters and ten slow fire shots in twelve minutes from standing at 200 yards, two minutes for two slow fire sighters followed by ten rapid fire shots in 60 seconds from sitting/kneeling at 200 yards, two minutes for two slow fire sighters followed by ten rapid fire shots in 70 seconds from prone at 300 yards, and two slow fire sighters followed by twenty record shots from prone in 22 minutes at 600 yards.

The 80-shot Regional Course simply adds ten more shots to the slow fire 200 yard standing stage, and adds another separate 10-shot string of rapid fire to both the 200 yard rapid fire stage and the 300 yard rapid fire stage. This game too requires highly precise equipment to be competitive, but you can actually show up with an M1 Garand, Springfield M1A, or AR15 in classic military M16 configuration and meet the rule requirement of "service rifle". Some sort of spotting scope, shooting mat, a padded glove for the support hand, a military M1907 sling (for service rifles), a jacket or sweatshirt, and a folding chair or stool are all required or helpful at one time or another.

Many ranges put on what they call "CMP" (Civilian Marksmanship Program) matches, which are the National Match Course, often shot at whatever reduced distance the range affords. Trying one of these at 100 or 200 yards is a great way to break into it.

These matches are edifying to watch. The better Smallbore shooters will put five shots from position at 50 yards into one hole the diameter of a pencil. The better Highpower shooters will hit quite well from standing on the 200 yard sev-en-inch 10-ring, and ditto from prone on the 12-inch 10-ring at 600 yards (this is where you really learn to read the wind).

This can also be intimidating to watch. Between the dollars invested in shooting coats, spotting scopes, and hand-built match rifles, the goofy side-shaded hats and sunglasses, and the distance to (and in some cases, the results on) the targets, a person can get faint.

Don't let this put you off, however. Have a talk with the shooters and the match crew and find out what it takes to at least give it a try. Often you will find someone happy to not only coach you, but loan you a spare rifle for the match. And some clubs will have regular clinics for new shooters to test the waters with borrowed equipment and good coaching. Such a clinic is a purely golden opportunity to try something new and rub shoulders with people who are "expert" and "master" at the game – and they'll be coaching you.

Metallic Silhouette shooting uses steel plate animal cut-outs for targets. In centerfire competition, chickens, pigs, turkeys, and rams are set up from 200 meters to 500 meters.

There is a bank of five of each animal type at its specified range. The shooter has to fire from standing, without a sling, and not only hit the steel but physically knock it down. If you want to be a better offhand shot, this is certainly the way to go. There is a rimfire rifle version of this, scaled down in target size and range (and there is a centerfire pistol version too).

Clubs affiliated with the U.S. Practical Shooting Association (USPSA) may hold what are called 3-gun matches. These are rifle/shotgun/pistol events geared more towards fast action, close range, multiple target type shooting that mirrors high-speed, high-round-count battle more than hunting. However, some of these clubs sometimes host a "manually-operated rifle" match where a basic scoped hunting rifle will be quite suitable, and the targets are further out and require careful shooting to hit. These are worth looking into if you can find one. Again, simply showing up to watch is a risk-free and logical first step.

Beyond this, there are many clubs that will often have informal matches of an endless variety. 100 yard egg shoots, deer target shoots, informal offhand shoots – there is no limit to the imagination of people looking to have fun and some friendly competition.

These are all chances to test your mettle, evaluate your hard-won skills under some varying degree of pressure, make new friends, and learn quite a bit in a friendly atmosphere. Don't be shy – go out and test the water!

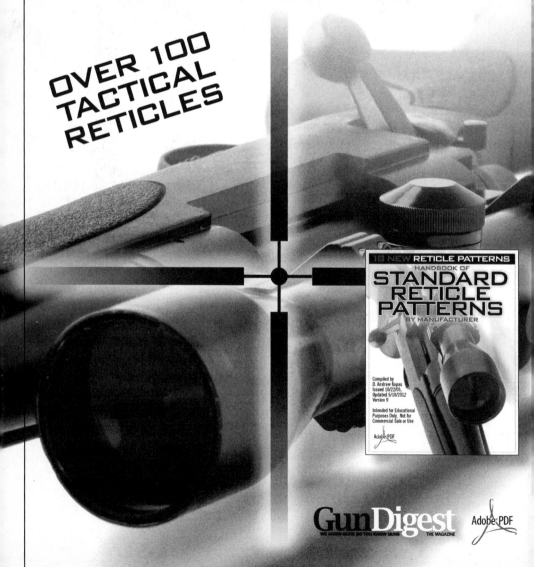